BROTHERS
in the
BELOVED
COMMUNITY

BROTHERS

in the

BELOVED
COMMUNITY

The Friendship of THICH NHAT HANH
and MARTIN LUTHER KING JR.

MARC ANDRUS

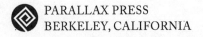

PARALLAX PRESS
BERKELEY, CALIFORNIA

Parallax Press
2236B Sixth Street
Berkeley, California 94710
www.parallax.org

Parallax Press is the publishing division of Plum Village Community of
Engaged Buddhism, Inc.

Cover design by Katie Eberle
Text design and composition by Happenstance Type-O-Rama

All reasonable efforts have been made to obtain permissions for every photograph included in this book.

ISBN: 978-1-946764-90-4

Library of Congress Cataloging-in-Publication Data is available.

1 2 3 4 5 / 26 25 24 23 22 21

To Sheila, for whom the
Beloved Community
is her true and constant home

Contents

Introduction

What would it be like to live in a place and time wherein humans experience the world as both full of meaning—with each person, each "being," a plenitude of beingness, each full of infinite wonder and beauty—and also as a world deeply interconnected? Such is not the world in which you and I were raised. Indeed, this enchanted world has been eroding for the last four hundred years. Today, when the depths of an individual being unfolds before me, and when the world shows its marvelous interrelated reality, I feel surprise, as it is such a contrast to the mechanistic, alienated world that is often our daily fare.

Brothers in the Beloved Community came to be because of several awakenings in my life over the last thirty years. If you have picked up this book, it seems probable to me that you may have shared these experiences, or at least some of them. Perhaps you have learned mindfulness from reading some of Thich Nhat Hanh's writings or by hearing him give one of his dharma talks. Or, perhaps Martin Luther King Jr.'s life and witness have given you courage and hope for racial justice, or, you have listened, with tears in your eyes, to Representative John Lewis's last message to the world, a message in which he spoke of the Beloved Community.

Beloved Community is a resonant and mysterious phrase, whose meaning beckons to us, but the content of which is not immediately apparent. Let me tell you how I came to love and respect Thich Nhat Hanh and Martin Luther King Jr.—and how I came to be committed to the Beloved Community that enlivened them. This story of discovery began while I served as a boarding school chaplain and moved forward in time to Alabama, California, and Vietnam. It is a story shining from two extraordinary lives with good news about how we might embrace a life more deeply connected and with capacity for transformation.

Peace Is Every Step

As a student in college, I walked back and forth each day between the agriculture campus, where I studied plants and soil, and the main campus, where I immersed myself in studying Eastern and African religions. Years later, browsing through the religion and philosophy section of a favorite bookstore, my attention gravitated to a slender paperback by an author I didn't know—Thich Nhat Hanh. The book was the newly published *Peace Is Every Step* (1990). I bought the book and took it back to the high school campus where I worked as a chaplain. Once I set foot on the campus, carrying *Peace Is Every Step*, something remarkable happened. Students, faculty, women and men working in the dining room—so many people—stopped me and asked me to tell them about this book. I concluded that we had a longing for peace and wanted to know about a book that offered guidance, a path to peace.

Not long after reading *Peace Is Every Step*, I learned that Thich Nhat Hanh was coming to give a dharma talk at the Washington National Cathedral. I took the metro into the city and made my way to the cathedral, joining the huge lines of people patiently waiting to get in. The cathedral was packed, but with an entirely new feel compared to the Christmas celebrations and sacred concerts I had attended there before. There was an energetic hush, a fullness of presence all around. Rather than clergy and choirs processing in to organ fanfare, there was one small person, Thich Nhat Hanh, seated on a cushion, quietly talking for about two hours. We were raptly attentive, hanging on every word in a connected, cohesive teaching discourse over that big chunk of time. The next year I went to hear Nhat Hanh again, this time at the Washington Hebrew Congregation. That sacred space also seats about five thousand people, like the National Cathedral—and like the cathedral, it was absolutely packed. That dharma talk, in 1993, was the last time I saw Thich Nhat Hanh in person until I made a pilgrimage to Vietnam as part of the research for this book in the spring of 2019—that journey is a story for later.

The Thich Nhat Hanh I met through *Peace Is Every Step* and those two dharma talks—as well as subsequent books and other dharma talks I listened to in videos—was the "monk who taught the world mindfulness," as a *Time* magazine headline described him. Helping millions of people learn to tend the good seeds in their souls through compassionate awareness is a great gift to humanity. I did not guess, however, that Thich Nhat Hanh's project of making Buddhist teachings on mindfulness, peace, and compassion available to broad swaths of the world's population was part of a bigger project, part of his commitment to the Beloved Community.

The Landscape Carries the Witness

I "met" Martin Luther King Jr. about a decade after reading Thich Nhat Hanh's *Peace Is Every Step*. In October 2001, I was elected bishop suffragan (an auxiliary bishop) for the Episcopal Diocese of Alabama, and my family and I moved to Birmingham in early 2002. I am a Southerner—I call myself a "pan-Southerner" in fact. I was raised in East Tennessee (yes, the three divisions of the state matter) by a North Carolinian mother and a Cajun father, and I lived in Virginia for twenty years. But actually moving to and living in the Deep South was something new to me.

For one thing, the history of the American civil rights movement was everywhere present, enduring in virtually every square foot of the city of Birmingham where we lived. The diocesan offices where I went to work each day were named Carpenter House, after C. C. Carpenter, who served the diocese as bishop for thirty years, a long episcopacy that spanned the crucial years of the civil rights movement of the 1950s and 1960s. In fact, Carpenter was one of the clergymen addressed by the Rev. Dr. Martin Luther King Jr. in his landmark "Letter from a Birmingham Jail" in 1963. King chose those seven white members of the clergy as the ostensible audience of his letter because they espoused "gradualism"—the idea that, yes, there should be equal rights for Blacks, but "not yet."

But while Bishop Carpenter was urging gradualism, others on his staff were working for civil rights. When I met Ambassador Andrew Young a number of years after our move to Birmingham, he asked me if an Episcopal laywoman in Birmingham, Peggy Roop, was still alive. I was startled that she was the first and only person Young asked about when he learned that I was a bishop from Alabama. Peggy Roop, a white woman who worked for the diocese as a coordinator of youth ministry in the 1960s, had opened, clandestinely, the very office in which I worked for important meetings between civil rights movement leaders and local white business people. Roop was in her early twenties then; her resolve and courage had deeply impressed Young. I was glad to tell him that she was alive and thriving. She was also quite modest—I had never heard this great story about her.

Other, similar stories of justice work by civil rights veterans became known with time, adding dimension to this remarkable place of living history, and there were material reminders as well.

Within walking distance of Carpenter House was the Sixteenth Street Baptist Church, where four Black girls were killed by a bomb detonated on a Sunday morning in 1963. Close to their church now stands the Birmingham Civil Rights Museum. Nearby is a park with statues that honor the young students who confronted police in nonviolent protest as part of the Children's Campaign. There are the students, arrested mid-stride in bronze, and there also are the snarling dogs and the police with high-pressure water hoses. And these are just the physical markers in Birmingham itself; the whole state is covered with reminders of the civil rights movement.

I increasingly viewed this location for my life and ministry in Alabama as a sacred landscape. The land was hallowed by the witness, the martyrdom of many Black people and their allies over many decades, even centuries. I began to hear a call—I needed to learn more, to get involved in the still-unfolding work of racial justice and reconciliation. It's a story that doesn't need recounting here in total, except to say that I not only began to read more and more about the movement and Black history, but I was also blessed to meet and learn from major veterans of the movement, such as the Rev. Dr. Vincent Harding, Ruby Sales, Catherine Flowers, Fannie Davis, the founders of the Lowndes County Black Panther Party, and others not as famous but so impressive to me.

King, though not the only leader of the movement, was more and more central in my understanding of the aims and values for which these heroes worked. King was not only a focal point for the movement, but his intellectual depth and prodigious energy also provided fuel to lead and propel the movement forward. Although his scope of understanding spread around the planet, he never lost sight of, or commitment to, the fundamental struggle for civil rights for Black Americans. And his influence in our common imagination has only increased with time. I came to view King as a "first among equals" among the many great civil rights leaders of the time.

The culmination of my experiences in Alabama in racial justice and reconciliation came just as we were leaving the state for a new life in California, where I had been elected the bishop of the Diocese of California (the Episcopal Church in the San Francisco Bay Area). In the heat of an Alabama August in 2006, I had the privilege to meet and hear Representative John Lewis speak at the closing Holy Communion service for the Jonathan Daniels and the Martyrs of Alabama Pilgrimage. This event was always stirring, bringing together people to Hayneville, the seat of Lowndes County, Alabama, to memorialize those who died while working for civil rights.

In his sermon, Congressman Lewis talked at some length about the Beloved Community. I had come across the phrase before—the Beloved Community—in King's writings and sermons and had found it both evocative and elusive. I was attracted to the idea without really knowing what its content was. Lewis, like King, linked the Beloved Community to nonviolence and reconciliation. Who is part of the Beloved Community? How do you enter the Beloved Community? Where is it? Is the Beloved Community an ideal, future state? Where did the idea of the Beloved Community begin, with King or with someone else? These were questions I carried with me, from Lewis's sermon to my life just beginning in California.

With these questions still alive and unanswered, I nevertheless made the Beloved Community the center of my stated hopes for the Diocese of California. I began an intensive study of the Beloved Community and the role that Thich Nhat Hanh and Martin Luther King Jr. played in advancing this reality, and I realized that their friendship—their brotherhood—was an embodiment, a manifestation of the Beloved Community itself. For more than fifteen years, while I've served as its bishop, the Diocese of California has joined me in seeking to both understand and embody the Beloved Community.

Journey to Vietnam

Once I learned that these two radiant beings, Martin Luther King Jr. and Thich Nhat Hanh, knew each other, supported one another, and had become friends, I began looking into the historical record of their interaction. The interlocking subjects related to their friendship are many, and each is vast: the Vietnam War, the American civil rights movement, the history of the Beloved Community, Vietnamese Buddhism, the nonviolent movement, the principles of Gandhian nonviolence—these are some of the relevant areas of study. Understanding Thich Nhat Hanh and King meant learning more about all of these while still keeping a focus on their friendship.

Friendship is more than outward action and expressions, more than, as the Christian scriptures say, "the body," meaning everything available to the senses. Friendship is a current of love that is spiritual, visible to what is called "the eyes of the heart." So it was when I learned, in the fall of 2018, that Thich Nhat Hanh had returned to Vietnam to live, after an exile that had begun more than fifty years before (he was exiled in 1966 for publicly speaking out against the war, and was permitted to visit in 2005), that I felt a tug to go there and pay my respects to him. I had research goals, yes, but more powerfully, I was drawn spiritually to make the trip, which I saw as a pilgrimage.

But this pilgrimage was not easy. Access to Thich Nhat Hanh was limited, communication with the monastic community there was spotty, and my work for the Episcopal Church was demanding and time-consuming. Twice I abandoned the idea. Finally, though, encouraged and helped by my family and a great friend, I went.

Thich Nhat Hanh now lives in the city of Hue, in the monastery that he had entered as a boy. I stayed at a pilgrimage hotel about two miles away. Every morning at five I got on my rented bicycle and made my way through the awakening city, which was, even in those early morning hours, already steaming at over ninety degrees Fahrenheit. Once at the monastery, I would join the nuns for walking meditation, then a silent, meditative breakfast, and then work—sweeping the patios, cleaning leaves out of the water-lily pool, and cleaning the breakfast dishes.

After these activities, the senior nuns gave me the priceless gift of hours of interviews. I soon realized that I was being given material that was precious beyond belief and known by virtually no one outside their small circle—for instance, that King passed on his understanding of the Beloved Community to Nhat Hanh in person, at their last meeting, in Geneva, Switzerland, in 1967, mere months before King's assassination.

The fruit of my pilgrimage to Vietnam, and of my pilgrimage through many books, articles, speeches, sermons, interviews, and letters, is this book, the biography of a friendship, the brotherhood of Martin Luther King Jr. and Thich Nhat Hanh.

A Biography of a Friendship

That a Vietnamese Buddhist teacher and peace activist and an American Baptist preacher and civil rights leader might become friends in the midst of a war raging between their countries—across not only political but religious barriers—was improbable. It may be surprising to you that I even call their relationship a friendship: Thich Nhat Hanh and Martin Luther King Jr. met in person only twice, each time for only a few hours. They exchanged some remarkable letters. King nominated Nhat Hanh for the 1967 Nobel Peace Prize and mentioned him (though not by name) in a landmark speech. Perhaps you'd think it best to call them collaborators.

Just the bare fact of their collaboration, though, floored me when I learned of it in 2014. The thought that these two had known each other, had worked with one another in the hope of bringing the Vietnam War to an end, and had felt warmly toward one another was a revelation to me.

I began researching their relationship, digging deeply into the small number of discrete artifacts that summed up the outer lineaments of their interaction—from the first letter, in 1965, from Nhat Hanh to King about the self-immolation of Buddhist monks to their last meeting, in Geneva, Switzerland, in 1967, just months before King's assassination. Each letter, each meeting was pregnant with meaning, brimming with new insights. But then I came across the following statement from Thich Nhat Hanh, made in 2014, before the massive stroke that has robbed him of speech and the ability to walk:

> *I was in New York when I heard the news of his assassination; I was devastated. I could not eat; I could not sleep. I made a deep vow to continue building what he called "the Beloved Community," not only for myself but for him also. I have done what I promised to Martin Luther King, Jr. And I think that I have always felt his support.*

This statement was a thunderclap for me. Numbers of questions came forth, the central ones being: In what way was Thich Nhat Hanh building the Beloved Community? And what did he mean that he felt King's support over all those years?

As I explored these questions, I came to the conclusion that for Thich Nhat Hanh, his relationship with King indeed continued and deepened beyond King's death, transforming from a collaboration of peace and justice advocates into friendship or even kinship, brotherhood. King has been extending his loving aid to Nhat Hanh over four decades, acting as, in the Buddhist understanding, a bodhisattva, a radiant being who devotes their energies to bringing enlightenment to all. In the Christian world, such a being might be called a "saint."

Equally affirming is the answer to the other question raised by Thich Nhat Hanh's 2014 statement, about the way in which he has kept his vow to continue building the Beloved Community. Scratch just a tiny bit below the surface of Thich Nhat Hanh's life history, and you could say that many of his commitments and efforts help manifest a restored Beloved Community: peace activism, anti-poverty programs in Vietnam, participation in rescue efforts for the Vietnamese boat people, work in promoting gender equality, environmental activism. It is, however, the work for which he is most famous that constitutes his most consequential contribution to building the Beloved Community, and it is a contribution that opens a way for us to join him in this work that is close at hand, available to us all, where we are now.

When Thich Nhat Hanh returned to live in Vietnam in 2018, the article about his homecoming in *Time* magazine called him "the monk who taught the world mindfulness" and "the father of mindfulness." At the core of Nhat Hanh's teachings about mindfulness is nonduality: as peace flowers in your heart, so it flowers in the universe. As the Beloved Community is repaired, built, manifested in your consciousness, so is it healed for all beings. Combining these two teachings—the pragmatic, lucid nature of Thich Nhat Hanh's teachings on mindfulness and his insistence that the Beloved Community is not to be found only in some heavenly realm, but right here in the messy, day-to-day life we all share—we can feel hope springing up in the face of overwhelming challenge.

Changing our perception, changing our inner landscape—nurturing the seeds of goodness within us—these acts change the world as truly as any other acts do. Referring to the climate crisis, the Emergence Network has posed this question: "What if our perception of the crisis *is* the crisis?" Put positively, by changing our perceptions, the fruit of mindfulness, we are making positive contributions to averting the planetary climate crisis. More general awareness of mindfulness and its importance is the gift that Thich Nhat Hanh has given the world to aid in building the Beloved Community.

Today, the United States is a divided country, one of many countries experiencing bitter, deep, and seemingly insurmountable divisions. We are divided over the treatment of immigrants from across our southern border. We are divided on race. We are divided on the reality of climate change. Whole regions of the country view other regions as being populated by people whose views are incomprehensible and indefensible. At a more intimate and smaller scale, families are divided, not able to speak freely on these polarizing issues with each other. In many cases, families are ruptured, relationships broken.

And yet the deepest desire of the universe is to connect. So said the late "geologian" Thomas Berry and cosmologist Brian Swimme in their groundbreaking book *The Universe Story*. We can feel the truth of their statement—that we want to connect with one another, with the earth, and for many of us, with the source of meaning: the divine. And yet we live in a world that is so broken, so marked by rupture. Our fractures create suffering whose scope we have difficulty in plumbing. Can we overcome the gulfs that divide us? Is there a path to healing, becoming whole?

I have come to believe that a way to fulfilling our deepest desire—the desire of the universe, the desire to connect—does exist. This healing way can be called *repairing the Beloved*

Community. Once I began to understand something of what the Beloved Community is, and how, once betrayed and broken, it can be healed, I committed to doing what I could to further this healing.

Perhaps you read the last words of the late congressman, John Lewis, who died in the summer of 2020, published in the *New York Times*. In that essay, Congressman Lewis wrote about when he first heard of the Beloved Community:

> *Like so many young people today, I was searching for a way out, or some might say a way in, and then I heard the voice of Dr. Martin Luther King Jr. on an old radio. He was talking about the philos- ophy and discipline of nonviolence. He said we are all complicit when we tolerate injustice. He said it is not enough to say it will get better by and by. . . . You must do something. Democracy is not a state [of being]. It is an act, and each generation must do its part to help build what we called the Beloved Community, a nation and world society at peace with itself.*
>
> *Ordinary people with extraordinary vision can redeem the soul of America by getting in what I call good trouble, necessary trouble.*

As one of the "ordinary people" of whom John Lewis wrote, I've learned, over the last fifteen years, that the "extraordinary vision" is present and here for us—we don't have to create it our- selves. I've also learned that there are many people lending their efforts to building the Beloved Community. There are literally millions of people living on Earth today who share this vision, though they may have other ways of naming it and other ways of contributing to its healing. Because the world is so marvelously interconnected, people pursuing different paths of justice—of getting into good trouble—are all contributing to the needed healing of the Beloved Community.

And I've also learned that the community of those com- mitted to the vision of the Beloved Community includes those radiant beings who have come before us in history. I now believe and know that Jesus and Buddha, Gandhi and King, Rosa Parks, and countless others are still at their work of compassion with us. Their contributions do not reside only in our memory but are as real now as my own acts.

Christians call such beings "saints," and Buddhists, "bodhisattvas." Among these saints, these bodhisattvas who join us in our work for justice and the building of the Beloved Community, there is a special power in the contribution of friends who undertake this work together. The witness of people who have come together despite barriers to friendship that seemed solid and unscalable has a strong, transformative quality. This book is about one of these remarkable friendships, that of Martin Luther King Jr. and Thich Nhat Hanh.

Viewed from today, we can see the qualities that drew Nhat Hanh and King together: their commitment to nonviolence; their spiritual grounding; the way they each in their own country worked to get religious people to come out of the safety of churches, temples, and monasteries and become active partners in societal transformation; the way each, during the course of that work, became world citizens. But before they met, I think the contrasts, the walls between them, would have been most obvious: their countries were locked in a war with each other; one was Christian, one Buddhist; one was a monk, one married; and they were of different races.

Throughout this book I have been guided by a decision to take two parts of Thich Nhat Hanh's 2014 statement with the utmost seriousness. First, I wanted to know what Nhat Hanh meant by saying he had kept his vow to maintain the Beloved Community across those decades since King's death. How had he kept this vow? Secondly, how had Nhat Hanh felt King's support during those intervening years—was it simply a function of memory, or by reading King's sermons and books? Or perhaps Nhat Hanh meant something about the ongoing presence of great beings who have died? In this last regard, I also wanted to know what it meant that Nhat Hanh told King in Geneva that "in Vietnam they call you a bodhisattva."

I have also tried to take the spiritual lives of both Thich Nhat Hanh and Martin Luther King Jr. as seriously as the record of their outward actions. King is often referred to as *Dr.* King, identifying him in a more secular fashion, without acknowledging him as an ordained Baptist minister. King, though, identified himself as a preacher, the son of a preacher, and the grandson of a preacher—his religious identity came first. So with King, I take into account his statements about prayer, for instance, as well as the ways he acted for peace and justice. To understand Nhat Hanh, I follow the same guidelines I have done for understanding King: paying attention to his religious statements with the same respect and curiosity I have for his peacemaking history. Thus, when Nhat Hanh calls King a bodhisattva, I want to peer into the meaning of this statement, ask what its implications are.

This book focuses on King and Nhat Hanh, but it will also place them in the context of the events and movements that were shaking the foundations of the world. The Vietnam War and the civil rights movement each in its own way heralded something new, both fissuring the solidity of the worldview of the time and presaging the future to come. The Vietnam War would be a defeat for the most powerful country on the planet and cause Americans to falter in their confidence. The civil rights movement raised the possibility that the supposed divide between subjects and objects could be breached and overcome—Black Americans could claim their equality and rights as subjects for the first time in America.

There was something else about to shake the foundations of the world, something not as obvious as the Vietnam War or the civil rights movement. A subterranean river of consciousness was about to flash and sparkle into the sunlight from its underground imprisonment—the Beloved Community was coming back into view. The Beloved Community was showing up in a new appreciation of interconnection itself. Suddenly, beginning in the mid-1950s and burgeoning through the 1960s, an interconnected worldview was flowering. In turn, the interconnected worldview was fueling new movements in the sciences, religion, and the arts. Systems ecology, Rachel Carson's clarion call in *Silent Spring*, James Lovelock's Gaia Theory, even Pope John XXIII's convening of Vatican II, were all clearly rooted in and drew upon a worldview that affirmed the interrelated structure of the universe.

The last book that Martin Luther King Jr. completed before his death was a book whose title and contents are as relevant today as they were in 1967: *Where Do We Go from Here: Chaos or Community?* On some level, all of us living in this moment of planetary threat recognize that our choices today are momentous. The call to action in 1967 by King was urgent, and the danger to the flourishing, perhaps even the existence, of life has burgeoned in the decades since then. The need for us all to take part in the repair of the Beloved Community has never been greater.

In the world of psychotherapy, a commonplace phrase is that it takes a person about as long to come out of a mental formation as it took to get into it. Extending this insight to a societal level, it is not hard to see why many people are despairing of being able to manifest the Beloved Community. It has taken roughly four hundred years to form the mechanistic worldview that prevails today. What are our hopes for undoing this disastrous worldview and building something better in the timeframe we have?

The brotherhood of Martin Luther King Jr. and Thich Nhat Hanh has much to teach us about the power that inheres in the Beloved Community. In this biography of their friendship, you will find grounds for hope for the changes that must be made to undo the mechanistic worldview. These changes will take the perseverance of effort across our lifetimes, as well as the efforts of those who follow us. James Howard Kunstler has called the threat of climate change the "long emergency," and climate change is one of the toxic byproducts of the mechanistic worldview. We will need to be at this work for the long haul. Metaphors drawn from wartime experience are not apt: once the war is "over," we will not be getting back to normal.

It will be well to recognize at the outset that the path into the Beloved Community is about transforming life, not solving a temporary problem. I hope that in reading this, you will find that we have help in this great work, the help of the holy people who have lived before us, the help of the Beloved Community itself. King's and Nhat Hanh's individual contributions to building the Beloved Community are prodigious. Their brotherhood, however, gives their contributions an added dimension. Loving bonds, however we name them, will guide us to the fullness of the Beloved Community. Indeed, they *are* the Beloved Community.

Thich Nhat Hanh and Martin Luther King Jr.,—brothers whose relationship has never ended, who are like subatomic particles entangled, bound together by the greatest force in the universe, unconditional love—can serve as our guides and companions as we make our own vows to continue the Beloved Community.

Lotus in a Sea of Fire

On June 12, 1963, many people around the world, including the president of the United States, opened their newspapers and looked with shock at a photograph of a Vietnamese Buddhist monk, Thich Quang Duc, seated cross-legged in a posture called the lotus position, engulfed in flame. Thich Quang Duc is composed and upright. The revered monk, in his mid-sixties, had been soaked in gasoline by a younger monk and had then struck a match to set himself on fire.

Thich Quang Duc immolated himself during the American war with North Vietnam and the Viet Cong. He was not protesting the war, but rather was calling attention to the repression of Buddhists by the South Vietnamese regime, which was allied with the Americans and the West. More monks and nuns followed Quang Duc in self-immolation, with five more dying that year and even more the next. These deaths were widely reported as "suicides" in the Western press, but they were viewed as a deep expression of commitment by Vietnamese Buddhists. Despite differences in interpretation, the self-immolations shook the consciousness of readers around the world.

For many religions, suicide is a grave sin. In the past, Christians of a variety of denominations who had taken their own lives were denied Christian burial and relegated to plots outside the consecrated cemeteries where their ancestors lay. Buddhism and Hinduism also believe that the souls of suicides suffer serious consequences in the afterlife. But these self-immolations, a young Buddhist monk named Thich Nhat Hanh argued, were not suicides, they were courageous acts of ultimate commitment and compassion.

In 1965, Thich Nhat Hanh, then unknown in America, wrote an open letter to the Baptist preacher and civil rights leader Martin Luther King Jr. In the letter, Nhat Hanh explained that the self-immolations of Buddhists in Vietnam expressed the highest spiritual values of compassion and courage. By explaining the meaning of the self-immolations, he was seeking to enlist King in the effort to bring peace to Vietnam. This letter, quoted in its entirety below, opened a door of much consequence in American and world history.

The self-burning of Vietnamese Buddhist monks in 1963 is somehow difficult for the Western Christian conscience to understand. The Press spoke then of suicide, but in the essence, it is not. It is not even a protest.

What the monks said in the letters they left before burning themselves aimed only at alarming, at moving the hearts of the oppressors and at calling the attention of the world to the suffering endured then by the Vietnamese. To burn oneself by fire is to prove that what one is saying is of the utmost importance. There is nothing more painful than burning oneself. To say something while experiencing this kind of pain is to say it with the utmost of courage, frankness, determination and sincerity.

During the ceremony of ordination, as practiced in the Mahayana tradition, the monk-candidate is required to burn one, or more, small spots on his body in taking the vow to observe the 250 rules of a bhikshu, to live the life of a monk, to attain enlightenment and to devote his life to the salvation of all beings.

One can, of course, say these things while sitting in a comfortable armchair; but when the words are uttered while kneeling before the community of sangha and experiencing this kind of pain, they will express all the seriousness of one's heart and mind, and carry much greater weight.

The Vietnamese monk, by burning himself, say [sic] with all his strength and determination that he can endure the greatest of sufferings to protect his people. But why does he have to burn himself to death? The difference between burning oneself and burning oneself to death is only a difference in degree, not in nature. A man who burns himself too much must die. The importance is not to take one's life, but to burn. What he really aims at is the expression of his will and determination, not death.

In the Buddhist belief, life is not confined to a period of 60 or 80 or 100 years: life is eternal. Life is not confined to this body: life is universal. To express will by burning oneself, therefore, is not to commit an act of destruction but to perform an act of construction, i.e., to suffer and to die for the sake of one's people. This is not suicide. Suicide is an act of self-destruction, having as causes the following:

> *lack of courage to live and to cope with difficulties*
>
> *defeat by life and loss of all hope*
>
> *desire for non-existence (abhava)*

This self-destruction is considered by Buddhism as one of the most serious crimes. The monk who burns himself has lost neither courage nor hope; nor does he desire non-existence. On the contrary, he is very courageous and hopeful and aspires for something good in the future. He does not think that he is destroying himself; he believes in the good fruition of his act of self-sacrifice for the sake of others. Like the Buddha in one of his former lives—as told in a story of Jataka—who gave himself to a hungry lion which was about to devour her own cubs, the monk believes he is practicing the doctrine of highest compassion by sacrificing himself in order to call the attention of, and to seek help from, the people of the world.

I believe with all my heart that the monks who burned themselves did not aim at the death of the oppressors but only at a change in their policy. Their enemies are not man. They are intolerance, fanaticism, dictatorship, cupidity, hatred and discrimination which lie within the heart of man. I also believe with all my being that the struggle for equality and freedom you lead in Birmingham, Alabama... is not aimed at the whites but only at intolerance, hatred and discrimination. These are real enemies of man—not man himself. In our unfortunate father land [sic] we are trying to yield desperately: do not kill man, even in man's name. Please kill the real enemies of man which are present everywhere, in our very hearts and minds.

Now in the confrontation of the big powers occurring in our country, hundreds and perhaps thousands of Vietnamese peasants and children lose their lives every day, and our land is unmercifully and tragically torn by a war which is already twenty years old. I am sure that since you have been engaged in one of the hardest struggles for equality and human rights, you are among those who understand fully, and who share with all their hearts, the indescribable suffering of the Vietnamese people. The world's greatest humanists would not remain silent. You yourself cannot remain silent.

America is said to have a strong religious foundation and spiritual leaders would not allow American political and economic doctrines to be deprived of the spiritual element. You cannot be silent since you have already been in action and you are in action because, in you, God is in action, too—to use Karl Barth's expression. And Albert Schweitzer, with his stress on the reverence for life and Paul Tillich with his courage to be, and thus, to love. And Niebuhr. And Mackay. And Fletcher. And Donald Harrington.

All these religious humanists, and many more, are not going to favour the existence of a shame such as the one mankind has to endure in Vietnam. Recently a young Buddhist monk named Thich Giac Thanh burned himself [April 20, 1965, in Saigon] to call the attention of the world to the suffering endured by the Vietnamese, the suffering caused by this unnecessary war—and you know that war is never necessary. Another young Buddhist, a nun named Hue Thien was about to sacrifice herself in the same way and with the same intent, but her will was not fulfilled because she did not have the time to strike a match before people saw and interfered. Nobody here wants the war. What is the war for, then? And whose is the war?

Yesterday in a class meeting, a student of mine prayed: "Lord Buddha, help us to be alert to realize that we are not victims of each other. We are victims of our own ignorance and the ignorance of others. Help us to avoid engaging ourselves more in mutual slaughter because of the will of others to power and to predominance." In writing to you, as a Buddhist, I profess my faith in Love, in Communion and in the World's Humanists whose thoughts and attitude should be the guide for all human kind [sic] in finding who is the real enemy of Man.

June 1, 1965
Nhat Hanh

Buddhist monastic novices, the letter said, made one or more small burns on their body as part of their ordination, demonstrating to themselves and their elders their commitment to their vows. The total self-burning, Nhat Hanh wrote, manifested total commitment. These Buddhists, like the civil rights activists in the United States, were throwing themselves "all in," not nullifying themselves. It is a hair-thin difference between the American activist who knowingly steps forward, again and again, into increasingly dangerous situations and the Buddhist monk or nun who lights the match that engulfs him or her in flames.

One of Nhat Hanh's early books, a history of Vietnam and the war in Vietnam, points to another interpretation of the self-sacrifice of Thich Quang Duc and those who followed him, beyond what Nhat Hanh unfolded in his letter to King. The cover of this book told a story that readers in Vietnam would have understood—the cover photo was of Quang Duc engulfed in flames. The title of the book was *Vietnam: The Lotus in a Sea of Fire*.

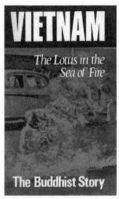

A subsequent paperback edition of the book held a less dramatic photo, though it was also taken at the scene of Quang Duc's self-immolation. This photo showed not Thich Quang Duc

Cover of the hardcover edition, published in 1967.

but some of the monks who accompanied him. They are bowing their heads toward the burning monk, illuminated by his death flames, their palms together, in a gesture of veneration. Together, what did this title and set of images mean?

During the French Vietnam War, which was ongoing from 1946 to 1954, the French began dropping an incendiary, napalm, on Vietnamese villages and forests. Napalm had been invented in the United States during World War II, and the US Army Air Force first used it in bombing raids over Berlin and Tokyo, where it caused mass destruction and terrified the population. Napalm was used again in the Korean War in the early 1950s, and the American military credited it with winning that war.

When the United States entered the Vietnam War, the use of napalm was continued and expanded. Between 1963 and 1973, the United States dropped 388,000 tons of napalm on Vietnam. One napalm bomb can destroy 2,500 square yards of space, setting off unquenchable flames. Because the bombs were dropped from fast-moving planes, accuracy was low—which resulted in many civilian deaths. The indiscriminate use of napalm was the "sea of fire" in Nhat Hanh's title.

In Buddhism, the lotus is a symbol of an enlightened being. The lotus flower floats serenely on the surface of the pond, but its stalk rises up through the water from a lakebed of mud. For Nhat Hanh, the beautiful lotus—enlightenment—never removes itself from its origins in the mud, the suffering of life.

In Vietnam during the 1960s, many Buddhist monks had a way of life that limited their contact with lay people. The majority of monks restricted their contact to their daily rounds collecting alms. Nhat Hanh was already, as a young monk, actively and theoretically challenging that prevailing pattern of Buddhist monastic life. A pioneer of what came to be called "Engaged Buddhism," he taught that enlightenment could be found in life's daily activities, at any moment. In each moment of life, a person—any person—might touch the Ultimate (enlightenment). Far from sullying the monastic, loving service to suffering people was taught by Nhat Hanh to be both "merit work," practices on par with sitting in meditation, practices that help awaken and free the monk, and the very channel to the experience of ultimate reality. Like Nhat Hanh's naming of Earth as a bodhisattva, the creation of Engaged Buddhism was a revolution in Buddhist thought and practice, far more than a simple shift in the field of activity for the monk.

For Thich Quang Duc, a revered elder monk, to walk to a public square, sit, be doused with gasoline, and then light himself on fire would have been understood by Nhat Hanh as the act of a bodhisattva, a being who vows to use their own awakening to bring enlightenment to all beings. Thich Quang Duc is the lotus in the midst of a world flaming with napalm, hatred, and incomprehension.

Who was this monk who sent his missive to Martin Luther King Jr., a message that originated in a culture and religion that must have registered as distant and deeply foreign to Christian ears? By 1965 Thich Nhat Hanh had been ordained as a Buddhist monk for twenty-three years, having become a novice monk at the age of sixteen.

Thich Nhat Hanh (born Nguyen Xuan Bao) was born in Hue, which was then the imperial capital of Vietnam. Pedaling along its streets today, you meet the smell of charcoal fires and cooking foods as you pass restaurants, shops, and shrines. The imperial complex has been preserved, a sprawling site with highly carved and painted wooden structures. Hue was (and still is) also a holy city, with many pagodas and associated monasteries.

An ardor for the Buddhist monastic life began to glow in Thich Nhat Hanh when he was eight or nine after he saw a painting of Gautama Buddha. He was struck by how peaceful the Buddha looked, a stark contrast to the world around him. Over the next few years, his feeling that he was meant to be a monk grew. When he was twelve, his elder brother, Nho, ordained as a monk. A few years later, at the age of sixteen, Thich Nhat Hanh ordained and began his novice training.

Thich Nhat Hanh's parents were unsure about their sons becoming monks. Although Thich Nhat Hanh was still young, as he grew into adolescence, he began to have ideas of how Buddhism, reformed and revived, could help Vietnam itself. As Thich Nhat Hanh's intention to ordain became more and more clear, he had conversations with his parents in which he started to express these views. Eventually, and with the path already blazed by his brother, they agreed that he could ordain and become a monk.

While I was in Vietnam as part of my research for this book, I shared a meal in a vegetarian restaurant with a group of senior nuns and young monks, all in the close circle around Thich Nhat Hanh. On the wall, surrounded by blooming plants, was a picture of the Buddha. Light emanated from his face and body. His smile was blessing us; I felt the Buddha's compassion and saw it mirrored in the faces of the kind people around me. Perhaps the picture of the Buddha that lit up young Nhat Hanh's heart was like this one, I thought.

From his earliest days of his budding intent to be a monk, Thich Nhat Hanh sought to refine, revive, preserve, and pass on the religious tradition of Vietnamese Buddhism. Ordaining women, breaking down the barriers between the monastic life and that of ordinary people, supporting the life of those living in poverty, he was to become a trailblazer in Southeast Asian Buddhism. His early dedication had a twin focus, both on monastic Buddhism and on his home country, Vietnam. Thich Nhat Hanh, like Martin Luther King Jr., eventually became a world citizen. Nevertheless, Nhat Hanh never abandoned his love of the people, the land, the flowers, the creatures of his home.

To track the many forms of Christianity, its astounding ram-ification, you need a large spreadsheet. Buddhism is less multi-form, but it does have several large branches, as well as schools and variants within them. The two main branches are Theravada and Mahayana. Vietnam's neighbors, like Myanmar and Thai-land, are centers of Theravada Buddhism, along with Sri Lanka and other places. Mahayana Buddhism is centered in China, Japan, Vietnam, Korea, and elsewhere.

The root form of Buddhism in India included a practice called *dhyana,* "concentration" or "meditation." As the Buddhist scriptures (sutras) were carried into China and translated, dhyana became *chan.* Chan Buddhism developed as a school within Mahayana Buddhism in China. Chan spread to Japan, where it is called Zen Buddhism, and to Vietnam, as Thien Buddhism. The sixteen-year-old Nhat Hanh became a monk in this Vietnamese Zen tradition, a form of Buddhism that de-emphasizes outward ritual (though not completely—forms of daily ritual, chanting, and special ceremonies remain important) and focuses on mindfulness as the central practice.

In addition to a focus on mindfulness practice, Thich Nhat Hanh as a young monk learned the main tenets of Mahayana Buddhism—that all of life is interconnected and that there are great beings who, within the web of life, convey compassion to all other beings, helping to free them from delusion and needless suffering. These light-filled beings are called bodhisattvas. Bodhi means "awake to the fullness of wisdom," and sattva is "being," so a bodhisattva is a being who embodies the wisdom of life. Compassion is at the heart of the wisdom of the bodhisattvas; their wisdom is never isolated or self-contained. Bodhisattvas exist to serve all beings. The interconnection of all beings and the role of the bodhisattva, these two key tenets of Mahayana Buddhism, as well as his Thien Buddhist practice of mindfulness, would be hallmarks of Thich Nhat Hanh's life for the next seven decades.

Tu Hieu, Thich Nhat Hanh's root temple where he first became a monk in 1942, is near Hue, a city in Central Vietnam. Hue is not only the historic imperial capital of Vietnam, it is a holy city, home to many pagodas and associated monasteries. One of those monasteries is Tu Hieu, which Nhat Hanh entered at sixteen to become a monk. The ancient pagoda is near a pond with lotus blossoms on its surface. As a young novice,

Nhat Hanh might have passed the pond often as he went about his daily activities or walked in meditation, as monks and nuns continue to do today. Nhat Hanh is now the unofficial abbott (not acknowledged by the Vietnamese government) at Tu Hieu today, at age 94, and has been living there since 2018.

Thich Nhat Hanh's lively intellect not only took him deep into the study of the dharma within conventional Buddhist study centers but also led him to be one of the first Vietnamese Buddhist monks to study in a secular Vietnamese university. The normal education of a monk might be better called "formation." It includes scholarly study of Buddhist scriptures and commentaries, but that study is set within a set pattern of activity within the monastery, each element of which—including meditation and the chanting of sutra text, so that they sink into the consciousness—transforms the devotee from the inside out. Without abandoning the monastic life he loved, Thich Nhat Hanh gave vent to his academic thirst as a university student. He enrolled in Saigon University and studied world literature.

After his university studies in Vietnam, Nhat Hanh continued to be a pioneer, traveling to undertake graduate studies at Princeton University and also teaching graduate seminars at Columbia University in 1962 and 1963. His strengths as a scholar were such that he was offered a teaching post at Columbia after the news leaked of his exile from Vietnam in 1966. While Nhat Hanh did not ultimately accept the position, the offer itself speaks to the esteem in which he was held by academic colleagues.

Thich Nhat Hanh whirled through life in the late 1950s and through the 1960s. Along with his academic work in Vietnam and the United States, he also founded a Buddhist university in Vietnam, several meditation centers, and a school of social work (School of Youth for Social Service, described in more detail on the following pages, as the school played such a key role in the creation of Engaged Buddhism), which trained young men and women, both ordained and lay, to work with the rural and urban poor.

During this period, Thich Nhat Hanh was also writing prolifically in a variety of genres: Buddhist teaching and apologetics, poetry, journals and memoirs, and even a play. When King nominated Nhat Hanh for the 1967 Nobel Peace Prize, he stated that Nhat Hanh was already the author of ten published volumes. The American Buddhist teacher and social activist Joanna Macy began her journey as a Buddhist following Nhat Hanh. Macy routinely calls him, first among her descriptions of him, a poet.

Who was the person, the still point, at the center of all this remarkable activity? One of Thich Nhat Hanh's longtime associates, Sister Chan Khong, who was a budding scientist in the late 1950s when she first met him, sheds light on this question. Born Cao Ngoc Phuong, Sister Chan Khong was both concerned for Vietnamese people living in poverty and seeking a deeper life as a Buddhist. She met with a prominent Buddhist monk, Thay Man Giac, and posed questions to him about the Buddhist life. Man Giac pulled out a book by Nhat Hanh and said, "The answer you are seeking is in this book." Chan Khong was frustrated, because what she wanted was a living discourse with the monk, not references to books. Trying to prod Man Giac into a conversation, Chan Khong kept asking questions. But each question was answered by reference to yet another Nhat Hanh book!

Finally, Chan Khong went to hear a lecture by Nhat Hanh. In her memoir, *Learning True Love*, she writes of that first encounter, "Thay Nhat Hanh impressed me deeply. I had never heard anyone speak so beautifully and profoundly." Chan Khong met Nhat Hanh after the lecture, but there wasn't time then—with other people wanting to speak to him—for her to ask him detailed questions. So she wrote him a letter:

> *I wrote and told him about my work and my dream of social change in Vietnam. I also expressed concern that most Buddhists did not seem to care about poor people. I said that I did not believe that helping poor people was merely merit work. In fact, I did not feel that I needed any merit for my next life. I wanted to help free people from their suffering and be happy in the present moment.**
>
> *Thay wrote back a kind letter, saying that he appreciated my work and that he would try to visit my project[†] one day. He said that he was sure a person could be enlightened by whatever kind of work he or she liked the most. "We should not be dualistic," he wrote. "We should just be ourselves and live our lives in the most mindful and deepest way we can." Later, he told me a story about a monk who spent much of his time sewing. One day, he was enlightened while mending an old robe. He had been doing it mindfully, with all his heart. If I like to help poor people, I could be enlightened by this work.[1]*

---

* "Merit work" refers to acts of charity that contribute to a practitioner's path to awakening and to liberation from the rounds of birth and death. When Chan Khong says that she didn't feel the need for merit work to advance her towards her next, better, life, she is expressing a belief that Nhat Hanh will reinforce philosophically—the Ultimate is available, can be "touched" in this life. While Nhat Hanh's teaching of what might be called "enlightenment now" ran counter to the prevailing practices of his day, he was not innovating within the great tradition of Buddhist thought, he was purifying and returning Buddhist thought to a deeply traditional stance. Gautama Buddha, in his life, was reacting to the Brahmanism of his time, questioning the need for social systems and practices that depended on a belief in slow growth in holiness through many lifetimes. Liberation, the Buddha taught, can be reached in one's own, current lifetime. In the end, acts of charity, Nhat Hanh would teach, are simply motivated by compassion, not as a means to an end.

† Chan Khong had already begun putting into practice her concern for Vietnamese people living in extreme poverty, creating a social service network that would later be formalized in Nhat Hanh's School of Youth for Social Service.

Living today, we might see Nhat Hanh's example (that of the monk who was enlightened while doing an ordinary household task) and the principle to which it points (that enlightenment is not reserved for those sequestered from the world) as obvious and commonplace, but it was unusual at the time.

By looking through Chan Khong's eyes, we are diving below the surface of Nhat Hanh's list of vast activities. Fortunately, we can also do that through reading his own self-understanding at the time—through the lyrical and honest *Fragrant Palm Leaves,* his journals from 1962 to 1966, which were begun when he was in the United States and finished in Vietnam. The Nhat Hanh who speaks from the pages of *Fragrant Palm Leaves* is not a two-dimensional image of a Buddhist monk, serene and unshakeable. Nhat Hanh is moved by beauty, particularly of nature—of plants, mountains, landscapes. He is touched by the kindness of friends. He feels loneliness and aches for his home country. Nhat Hanh is so heartbroken by the opposition he and his fellow reformers and social activists experience from the Vietnamese Buddhist hierarchy that he becomes dangerously ill, fevered and unable to eat.

> *We felt lost. Our opportunity to influence the direction of Buddhism had slipped away. The hierarchy was so conservative. What chance did we—young people without position or a center of our own— have to realize our dreams? I became so sick I almost died, so I left the city to live in a small temple in the Blao province. Our other friends also scattered to the winds. It felt like the end.[2]*

Nhat Hanh describes being overtaken by inner spiritual battles in which he is battered and left tattered and devastated:

> *Sometimes I feel caught between two opposing selves—the "false self" imposed by society and what I would call my "true self." How often we confuse the two and assume society's mold to be our true*

self. Battles between our two selves rarely result in a peaceful rec-
onciliation. Our mind becomes a battlefield on which the . . . form,
feelings, perceptions, mental formations, and consciousness of our
being . . . are strewn about like debris in a hurricane. Trees topple,
branches snap, houses crash. These are our loneliest moments, . . . but
when such a frenzied hurricane strikes, nothing outside can help. I
am battered and torn apart, and I am also saved.

I passed through such a storm this past autumn. It began in
October. At first it seemed like a passing cloud. But after several
hours, I began to feel my body turning to smoke and floating away.
I became a faint wisp of a cloud. I had always thought of myself as
a solid entity, and suddenly I saw that I'm not solid at all. . . . My
true nature, I realized, was much more real, both uglier and more
beautiful than I could have imagined.

Finally, Nhat Hanh is visited by beloved figures who have
died in his past.

The full moon of October. My mother was with me. No doubt she
had followed me to the temple as the moon was first peeking over
the horizon. As I listened to the sermon and then to Kimioto's music,
the moon shone on the temple roof, and now it followed me home.
My mother died six years ago on the full moon day of October. The
midnight moon is as gentle and wondrous as a mother's love. For
the first four years after she died, I felt like an orphan. Then one
night she came to me in a dream, and from that moment on, I no
longer felt her death as a loss. I understood that she had never died,
that my sorrow was based on illusion.

Thich Nhat Hanh in the late 1950s and the 1960s may have
been a juggernaut of outward activity, making admirable and
abundant accomplishments, but at the same time, his inner life
was steadily growing. We are fortunate that Nhat Hanh committed to a journal his inner thoughts in the midst of an intense
outward life. For instance, here is a passage where Nhat Hanh

writes about the war and its effect on him and his circle of Buddhist friends and followers:

> *In Vietnam, the war is escalating. Our people are caught between a hammer and an anvil. We've lost so much already. The country has been divided in two and engulfed in flames. Even Phuong Boi* is fading into the fog. But as long as we have each other, we can never be truly alone. We want to stand with those who have been abandoned. I want others, at least occasionally, to turn their thoughts to those who suffer—to think about them but not pity them. Those who suffer do not want pity. They want love and respect.[3]*

Nhat Hanh joined and soon became a leader in the war's peace movement in Vietnam. His effort to build peace took several forms, through combating poverty and using his creative skills as a writer—both in poetry and discursive historical writing. From the start, Nhat Hanh applied his philosophic commitment to nondualism to his peace activities. He saw Vietnam as one country, united, and he rigorously stayed away from advocating for victory for either the Communist North or the U.S.-aligned South. Nondualism—looking at the whole rather than choosing one subgroup over another—and nonviolence guided Nhat Hanh's peace activities throughout the Vietnam War, and they have continued to shape his life in the decades since then.

In Sister Chan Khong's memoir, where she describes their first exchange of letters, she says that Nhat Hanh applied the doctrine of nondualism also to the traditional divide between Buddhism and the rest of the world:

---

* A retreat center in Vietnam's Central Highlands that Nhat Hanh and several friends built in the 1950s. "Phuong Boi" means "Fragrant Palm Leaves," the English name of a published volume of Nhat Hanh's journals from the early 1960s. Phuong Boi was very dear to Nhat Hanh.

He said that I was not alone [in being interested both in exploring Buddhism more deeply and in working for social change], that he had seen many efforts by Buddhists to help the sick and the poor in other parts of Vietnam. [He] believed that Buddhism had much to contribute to real social change.

At the time, however, this stance was not only unusual, but one that could provoke censure from the Buddhist authorities in Vietnam.[4] In January 1964, Nhat Hanh submitted a proposal to the executive council of the recently founded Unified Buddhist Church (UBC), which united all of the Buddhist traditions in Vietnam. The proposal had three points:

1. The church should publicly call for cessation of hostilities in Vietnam.

2. The church should help build an Institute for the Study and Practice of Buddhism to train the country's leaders to practice the tolerant, open-minded spirit taught by the Buddha and sorely needed by the nation.

3. The church should develop a center for training social workers to help bring about nonviolent social change based on the Buddha's teachings.[5]

The Buddhist authorities endorsed only the second point of the proposal.[6] Nhat Hanh, however, supported by many young adults, including Sister Chan Khong, moved ahead with the effort to create a center for training social workers, and in 1965, the School of Youth for Social Service (SYSS) was founded.[7]

The School of Youth for Social Service trained young adults to build capacity for ordinary Vietnamese citizens to make them independent of the vagaries of government programs and to help them recover from the devastation of the war with France and the new conflict with the United States. The students, mostly lay Buddhists, along with some monastics, enrolled in a two-year training program that equipped them to both provide direct social services and to share their own training, passing it on to people living in poverty. Two hundred students out of the three hundred who applied (the limitation was due to the capacity of the school's infrastructure) were admitted to the first class in 1965.

Students at the university that Nhat Hanh founded, Van Hanh University, issued a declaration calling for peace in 1965. The peace declaration kept the country as a whole in view, rather than choosing one side over the other, showing Nhat Hanh's influence:

It is time for North and South Vietnam to find a way to stop the war and help all Vietnamese people live peacefully and with mutual respect.

This simple statement calling for peace for all of Vietnam conceals a deep philosophical commitment within Buddhism to nondualism. By contrast, dualism, or binary thinking—wrong and right, yes and no, even the power of computer coding language with one and zeros at their base—can have adverse social outcomes. People line up on one side of the binary equation or the other; for instance, in an extreme condition of dualism, binary thinking, there can be no common ground between political parties. In such a charged environment, governance can be paralyzed. A nondual approach like Nhat Hanh's can advance the causes of peace by holding all possible "sides" in one frame, united by love.

American commentators, as they met or read about Thich Nhat Hanh, declared he either was or emphatically was not a Communist, though Nhat Hanh himself carefully avoided laying blame or taking sides in his writings. The end result was that both sides disapproved of him, and in 1966 he was exiled and found it impossible to return to his beloved homeland.

Global trends—European colonialism that entrained Christianity, as well as the Cold War struggle between the United States and Communist Soviet Union and the People's Republic of China and their allies—all converged on Vietnam, creating the bitter conflict that Thich Nhat Hanh tried to heal. Against the intense pressure of these geopolitical forces, Thich Nhat Hanh marshaled his own mindfulness, the power of his community (sangha), and one other invisible power to resist and to transform. This power, real but unseen, was the compassion of bodhisattvas. Thich Nhat Hanh drew on their strength in a concrete way by reaching out to someone he had called a bodhisattva: Dr. Martin Luther King Jr.

Moving into the World House

Who was Martin Luther King Jr. leading up to the first communication between him and Thich Nhat Hanh—the letter in which Nhat Hanh explained the self-immolation of Buddhist monks in the early 1960s and sought King's help in opposing the Vietnam War? King has since become such a towering figure that his popular portrait can sometimes seem something of a caricature, or at least a portrait so simplified that it is misleading. The portrait of King in what follows is also somewhat broad-brush—other sources will more nearly approach full biographies of King.

Martin Luther King Jr. was deeply inculcated in the Baptist Church. Perhaps wryly reversing the statement of the prophet Amos, he said of himself, "I am a preacher, the son of a preacher, the grandson of a preacher and the great-grandson of a preacher."*

King attended one of the leading Black colleges, Morehouse, in Atlanta, beginning at the age of fifteen. Graduating

---

* King is making a wry reference to the great Hebrew prophet Amos, who claimed (Amos 7:14), "I am not a prophet nor the son of a prophet," meaning he was not a member of the professional bands of prophets who held court positions at the time. Amos was the source of one of King's favored biblical quotations, "Let justice roll down like waters, and righteousness like an everlasting stream."

from Morehouse at nineteen, King followed in the footsteps of his father and grandfather and was ordained as a minister at Ebenezer Baptist Church, and then traveled north to continue his education at Crozer Theological Seminary, outside of Philadelphia. Crozer was considered the most progressive seminary in the United States at the time. The bachelor of divinity degree that King earned at Crozer was both intellectually rigorous and provided a practical basis for ministry. A case in point is preparation for preaching—for which King became justifiably famous. While at Crozer, King took an astonishing eight courses on preaching. This course load is all the more remarkable in light of current seminary courses of study—today, the Southern Baptist Theological Seminary in Louisville, Kentucky, offers two courses in preaching, which is typical for American seminaries. Harvard Divinity School, out of a dizzying set of course listings—close to 250 different courses—has only two courses on preaching, one of which is specifically for preaching in the Unitarian-Universalist tradition, and neither of which is required. After seminary, King went on to earn a doctorate at Boston University, and while he is more commonly referred to as Dr. King than identified as a Christian minister, it is important to remember that all of his most important speeches were, in fact, sermons, and they were often delivered in houses of worship.

This preacher of the Gospel, following his family tradition, honed both his understanding of the Christian scriptures and how to convey the virtues and qualities enshrined in those scriptures to the people of the local church. How should the community meet challenge, suffering, and oppression? Where is hope in the midst of looming shadow? King had prepared himself to answer these serious, vexing existential questions for the Black church, brought home in the lives of the ordinary men, women, and children in the congregations King served in Alabama and

Georgia. King surely knew well how, in the biblical story of the young shepherd, David, upon whom God thrusts the burden of kingship, the tools and skills acquired for one vocation—shepherding his father's sheep—are turned to other ends, first overcoming the Philistine champion, Goliath, in one-on-one combat, and later shepherding the people of Israel. Just so, King turned the skills of preaching and congregational leadership to the engagement of an evolving social movement to bring justice for Black America.

To understand Martin Luther King Jr. in the years leading up to his meeting with Thich Nhat Hanh, we can't lose sight of his identity as a Black Baptist minister. Against the backdrop of local church leadership, King's ascendency as a leader of a mass movement aimed at transforming civil society appears all the more remarkable. The success of King's leadership of the civil rights movement was not, however, divorced from the Black church, but instead was based on mobilizing the church and forging partnerships between devout Christians and secular allies.

Introduced to the philosophic school of personalism first at Morehouse and then, in more depth and detail, at Crozer, King moved to Boston and entered the doctoral program in systematic theology at Boston University, a preeminent center for personalism studies. Personalism, and its importance for King, can be best understood in the light of diverse philosophic developments in Enlightenment thought, currents that de-emphasized the importance of the personal and lifted up more abstract forces and principles as operating and shaping reality. By contrast, personalism re-centered the importance of the human person, and of the Divine having personhood as well. King believed passionately in the dignity and work of the human person and in the beneficent agency of a loving God, a God with personhood who actively aided the suffering and oppressed people in the world.

It was in Boston that the young doctoral student was introduced to the remarkable Coretta Scott, who was studying vocal music performance at the New England Conservatory of Music. Scott played a variety of musical instruments, sang, and acted in musical theater, and she was already active in the growing civil rights movement. Before meeting Martin King, she was involved in the NAACP at Antioch college where she did her undergraduate work. Her elder sister, Edythe, was the first Black student at Antioch—the Scotts were not only activists, but groundbreakers.

As with Martin Luther King Jr.'s religious commitments, the contributions of Coretta Scott King—not only to her husband's success but also to the success of the civil rights movement—are often underemphasized or completely overlooked. For example, Coretta Scott King personally intervened with the young Massachusetts senator and candidate for the American presidency, John F. Kennedy, to gain his help in freeing her husband from a jail sentence of four months of hard labor. King also used her musical training and talent to give concerts that did what art does better than any other medium—change and charge the hearts of the listeners to understand and join a cause. Coretta Scott King was part of the 1959 trip to India, and she enthralled huge crowds there with her singing, helping forge the relationship between the nonviolent activists in India and those in the United States.

Debbie Elliott, a writer for National Public Radio, expresses well the power of Scott King as an activist, apart from her husband, and the equal of any of the other prominent civil rights leaders:

> But her presence in Memphis, Tenn., just four days after her husband was slain there, was the act of a civil rights leader in her own right.
>
> On April 8, 1968, Coretta Scott King wore a black lace headscarf as she led a march through downtown Memphis. Three of her four children were at her side.

"I was impelled to come," she said at the time. "I ask the question, 'How many men must die before we can really have a free and true and peaceful society?'"

"I just think that that was one of the most incredibly brave acts in my lifetime," says Clayborne Carson, a professor of history and director of the Martin Luther King Research and Education Institute at Stanford University.

"To have the courage to go back to the place where her husband was assassinated with her kids and with the history of the previous violence that had brought Martin back to Memphis," he says.[8]

Today, Martin Luther King is a towering figure in the history of the civil rights movement. His stature often overshadows the more nuanced, diverse texture of the movement for which he became the most famous face and voice. There were many other leaders, dispersed in a number of groups or cells. Ori Brafman and Rob Beckstrom, in their book *The Starfish and the Spider*, compare two kinds of organizational models. One, the "starfish" model, is a cellular structure with no central leader and is a more enduring, effective form for a social movement than the "spider" model, which is powerful but is overly reliant on one leader. The book says that while the starfish model is potent, the model that lasts the longest and makes the biggest impact is a hybrid model.

The hybrid model is just what the civil rights movement was: having a central head but with semi-autonomous cells. King emerged as the focal point, an inspiring preacher who captivated and catalyzed mass gatherings and a keen strategist who was able to forge a dynamic coalition from people holding diverse views and commitments. The structure of the movement as a whole, however, was far more freewheeling and horizontally structured than is commonly understood.

For one thing, most of the leaders in the public consciousness of the civil rights movement were men (Coretta Scott King herself criticized the movement for its male-dominated leadership). In part, this reflected wider societal attitudes—Martin himself expected that Coretta would abandon her own career to be a mother and housewife. But in fact, there were many women active in and acting as leaders in the civil rights movement. Fannie Lou Hamer, Rosa Parks, Coretta Scott King, and Ella Baker are just a few. In addition to the previous highlighting of Coretta Scott King, it will balance and enrich an understanding of King's position to illuminate three of these women civil rights leaders: Hamer, Parks, and Baker.

Fannie Lou Hamer was ill-educated, a stark contrast to King's undergraduate, divinity, and doctoral degrees. Hamer loved learning but was forced to begin working early by the necessity of aiding her family in their concerted attempts to scrape by economically in racist Mississippi. The youngest of twenty children in a sharecropper family, Hamer had to leave formal schooling after the sixth grade. Thirsting after learning, Hamer continued to read voraciously in the Bible. During her years of activism, listeners marveled that she could quote long passages of scriptures that supported the cause of justice, while at the same time both Blacks and whites ridiculed her for her heavy southern accent and poor grammar.

Disdain and worse didn't stop Hamer, however, once the Black civil rights movement arrived in Sunflower County and she learned that she could gain the power of the vote. Not content with gaining her own voting rights, Hamer began to organize others and entered the sphere of Democratic Party politics in Mississippi. A highpoint of Hamer's political organizing was her speech at the 1964 Democratic Party Convention. Hamer insisted that the Black Freedom Democratic Party be officially seated to represent Mississippi at the convention. In her speech she recounted the fateful day when she and others from Ruleville

(in Sunflower County) went by bus to the county seat to register as voters. A racist, voter suppression policy was enforced, by
which Black voters had to pass a literacy test.

After registering, being brought back to the country seat
by police and highway patrol and experiencing harassment
there, Hamer was threatened by the plantation owner, who said
to her, "'We are not ready for that [Black voter registration]
in Mississippi.' I addressed him and told him, 'I didn't try to
register for you, I tried to register for myself.'" At the end of
her speech, she declared, "If the Freedom Democratic Party is
not seated [at the convention] I question America. Is this the
land of the free and the home of the brave? Where we have to
sleep with our telephones off the hook because we be threatened daily, because we want to live as decent human beings in
America. Thank you."

Plagued by ill health as a result of unceasing, back-breaking
work (in the cotton fields for many years) and poor access to
health care, Hamer died at age sixty, somewhat alone and believ-
ing she had not made a significant difference for this same
America and especially for Black people in America. Resignedly
she said, "I'm sick and tired of being sick and tired." Contrary to
what she thought in her dying days, Hamer had a great influence
on the civil rights movement, and she is remembered for her
contributions more than forty years later.

Ella Baker was of an older generation than Hamer and King,
born in 1903, but her life spanned eighty-three years; she died in
New York City in 1986. Baker graduated from Shaw University
in North Carolina, the second oldest Historically Black College
and University in the United States. Born in Virginia, Baker was
raised on a farm in North Carolina, where one of her grand-
mothers, who had been born in slavery, lived with them. From
this grandmother Baker heard first-hand accounts of the horrors

of slavery, stories that set her on the path of being a civil rights activist, and also a feminist.

Baker was a woman of faith, but critiqued the Black church as being supported by women but dominated by men. Far from the boon that many have seen in the Black church providing so many leaders in the civil rights movement of the '50s and '60s, Baker saw a continuity of male domination and top-down leadership from the Black church to the Black civil rights movement. As a focal point of both church and movement, King came in for some of Baker's criticisms.

Instead of top-down leadership, Baker promoted radical democracy, building power from the ground up. She founded the Student Nonviolent Coordinating Committee on the campus of her alma mater, a more raucous organization, pressing more intensely for social change than the older NAACP. She and King together founded the Southern Christian Leadership Conference, of which King became the head. Baker and King's relationship was emblematic of the politics of the movement— there were disagreements, sometimes great, but they "kept their eyes on the prize." One of Baker's oft-quoted statements that encapsulates her radical democracy and her spirituality was learned from her parents, "Lift as you climb."

The story of Rosa Parks and the Montgomery Bus Boycott is further illustrative. King and his wife had arrived in Montgomery in 1954, where King had accepted the pastorate of the Dexter Avenue Baptist Church. They were only recently married, and King was only twenty-five years old.

On December 1, 1955, Rosa Parks refused to give up her seat to a white rider on a Montgomery bus and was arrested, jailed, and fined. Some accounts of Parks's history-making action have portrayed her as simply being too tired to get up and move—tired from work and tired from the cumulative effects of discrimination, the sorrow of all the suffering and death visited upon Blacks by white America. The truth tells a great deal about the reality of the civil rights movement. Parks had been a part of the civil rights movement since the early 1940s, when she joined the Montgomery chapter of the National Association for the Advancement of Colored People (NAACP)—and became the chapter's secretary. Furthermore, four months before her arrest, Parks had attended a training session for civil rights activists at the Highlander Folk School (later called the Highlander Research and Education Center) in the mountains of Tennessee. Connecting to Highlander in itself broadened Parks's activism network and honed her skills in nonviolent protest.

In addition to Highlander and the NAACP, another organization that played a critical role in the Montgomery Bus Boycott was the Women's Political Council. The Women's Political Council (WPC) distributed flyers around Montgomery promoting the boycott that began five days after Parks was arrested, and Jo Ann Robinson, WPC president, organized the boycott.

It was in the rich mix of organizations and activists around Rosa Parks that King—then twenty-six years old—was chosen to be the boycott leader. King was a center point in a complex network that collectively is known as the civil rights movement. Understanding King in this more nuanced role helps us see him more truly in the years leading up to his first communication with Thich Nhat Hanh in 1965.

As with Nhat Hanh's growth toward world citizenship, experiences in King's life of suffering and of positive opportunity helped open him up to an expanded, global sense of his "location" in the world. One of these experiences was the journey the Kings made to India in 1959. In making this trip, King was following in the footsteps of Howard Thurman, whom King acknowledged as a model and mentor.*

Thurman is a paradoxical figure in the history of the civil rights movement in the twentieth century. Forceful and clear about the use of social pressure tactics like boycotts, at the same time Thurman was known as a mystic. As a child in the Panhandle of Florida, Thurman was entranced and thrilled by the overwhelming power of hurricanes, feeling through them the power of God. Thurman gave his natural mysticism an intellectual underpinning by studying with Quaker philosopher Rufus Jones during graduate work at Haverford College.

Thurman made a ground-breaking trip to India in 1935, which paved the way for other Black religious and academic leaders, such as Benjamin Mays, to make their own journeys of discovery around nonviolent protest and action. What set Thurman's trip apart from those that followed was not only that it was the first of a series, but also that Thurman and his companions were able to meet and talk with Gandhi himself. Thurman arrived in India in late 1935 and met with Gandhi in early 1936.

Thurman had already been introduced to the principles of nonviolence through his membership in the Fellowship of Reconciliation and by one of its earliest leaders, minister and union organizer A. J. Muste (who will be discussed in more depth later). Gandhi, however, enriched Thurman's understanding of nonviolence greatly by expounding principles of nonviolence that he had received from within Hinduism and refined through his leadership of the Indian independence movement. Principles

---

* After founding and leading the first interfaith church in the United States, the Church for the Fellowship of All Peoples, Thurman became the dean of the chapel at Boston University. It was at BU that Thurman met King, then in the last years of his doctoral studies.

such as ahimsa (nonviolence) and satyagraha (literally holding onto truth) became part of the working vocabulary of the civil rights movement.

Other leaders of the civil rights movement also continued to expand the understanding of nonviolence, drawing more and more from the well of the India-based movement Thurman had encountered in his 1935 trip. One of these leaders whom King relied on—who began advising King on Gandhi and nonviolence in the mid-1950s—was Bayard Rustin. Rustin, always frank about being a gay man, didn't want his sexuality to draw attention and energy away from the civil rights movement, and he therefore worked more often behind the scenes. Though less in the limelight than many of King's associates, Rustin was an active force in helping King cultivate an American, Black version of Gandhian nonviolence.

When the Kings made their journey to India in 1959, they learned first-hand of the great nonviolent movement that had removed the British colonial control of the subcontinent after two centuries of rule. That the mission of *swaraj* (self-governance) was nonviolent and was a movement of people of color inspired King; what was possible in India might come to be in the United States. King was interviewed in India on that trip, and he said, "Since being in India, I am more convinced than ever before that the method of nonviolent resistance is the most potent weapon available to oppressed people in their struggle for justice and human dignity."[9]

Events of terror and sorrow also continued to galvanize King, moving him away from plans to work as an academic or a Baptist minister in the nonpolitical mold. In 1963 King and the wider world witnessed the assassination of Medgar Evers and the bombing of the Sixteenth Street Baptist Church in Birmingham, Alabama, which claimed the lives of four elementary-school girls.

Both of those events were acts of terrorism meant to frighten the burgeoning civil rights movement. The killing of Evers not only sent shock waves through the Black and civil rights communities but also removed an important leader of the movement. Evers, just thirty-seven years old when he died, was a World War II veteran, college graduate, and civil rights activist.

As field secretary for the NAACP, Evers publicly investigated the 1955 murder of fourteen-year-old Emmett Till. He also organized a boycott of gas stations in his region of Mississippi that wouldn't allow Blacks to use their restrooms and worked with James Meredith to integrate the University of Mississippi. His prominence led to violent attacks by white supremacists. Finally, on July 12, 1963, avowed racist Byron Beckwith hid in bushes near Evers's home in Jackson, Mississippi, where his wife, Myrlie, and three children were anxiously waiting for him. As Evers walked from his car toward his house, Beckwith shot him. Evers struggled forward and collapsed at his front door. His wife found him moments later.

The same year, King himself was jailed for the thirteenth time for his civil rights activism, this time in Birmingham. King was treated harshly during this jailing and was held in solitary confinement. The cumulative pressure of the violence and suffering amalgamated with King's brilliance and passion and one of the landmarks of twentieth-century English literature emerged—his "Letter from a Birmingham Jail."

The letter is a treasure, containing clear pictures of King's philosophy and strategy of nonviolence. Unpacking this letter will help us understand the King who blazed into the world's sight. It contains an early statement of King's belief in the interconnectedness of life, a quality of reality that is at the heart of the Beloved Community. Whenever King mentioned the Beloved Community in his writing, sermons, and speeches, he

also speaks of reconciliation. The letter is an attempt at reconciliation, calling for the restoration of the Beloved Community.
In the letter, King opens a window into a spiritual practice in
nonviolent activism (self-purification) and a strategic practice
("raising the tension") that he derived from the teachings of
the ancient Greek philosopher Socrates. More than merely discussing these tactics in the letter, King uses the letter to deploy
them. King raises the tension for the seven members of the
clergy to whom he addressed the letter, a tactic that worked in
the case of one of these men. Finally, King uses the letter itself
as part of a well-thought-out direct action: the letter and the
Birmingham Campaign are really two parts of one great nonviolent action.

The Beloved Community is a community not only in which
all are included and all are at peace with one another, but also
one in which each being in the community is connected to every
other being. In places where the Industrial Revolution and the
associated economies have created the conditions for hyper-
individualism, it can be hard to grasp what an interconnected
world is like. For King, it meant that each part of the whole,
and the whole itself, suffers when even the smallest, seemingly
most insignificant part suffers. The letter is an early statement of
King's belief in the interconnectedness of life:

> *I am cognizant of the interrelatedness of all communities and
> states. I cannot sit idly by in Atlanta and not be concerned by
> what happens in Birmingham. Injustice anywhere is a threat to
> justice everywhere. We are caught in an inescapable network of
> mutuality, tied in a single garment of destiny. Whatever affects
> one directly affects all indirectly. Never again can we afford to live
> with the narrow provincial "outside agitator" idea. Anyone who
> lives in the United States can never be considered an outsider any-
> where in this country.*

The *conscious* recognition of life's interconnectedness is central to how the Beloved Community is defined. It would be fair to say that closing the gap between reality (the interconnectedness of all being) and how we commonly live (as if there are beings so far below one in status that they can be used, as natural resources are used) is fundamental to the letter. You could say that the interconnected world is the original state of the world, its Edenic, primal origin. The great world religions have all, ideally, affirmed this interconnectedness, though in the modern era not all religions see other species and Earth itself as sharing in this blessed quality of interconnectedness. Reconciliation, King wrote again and again, is the path (along with nonviolence) to the Beloved Community. In his letter, King is attempting to bring a group of white ministers "across the gap," to help them be reconciled.

King addressed the letter to seven members of the clergy, six Christian and one Jewish. The immediate reason he wrote these particular men is that they themselves (along with an eighth man) had issued their own letter in the weeks before King was jailed, in which they urged Blacks in Birmingham to reject King's leadership, painting him as an outsider and, even more fundamentally, asking that Birmingham residents turn away from nonviolent protest and patiently wait for promised reforms to take place. The clergy's position—reform is needed, but now is not the time—has been labeled "gradualism," and King's letter exposes its hollowness, showing how promise after promise of reform had been broken.

There is a deeper reason that King addresses his letter to these seven men, though, a reason bound up with the reality of the Beloved Community and the work of reconciliation. King writes to them as faith leaders in the Judeo-Christian heritage. And he writes to them as one of them, a Christian minister, but as a Black man, and from a jail cell.

These ministers had all formally, by their ordinations in their respective religions and denominations, pledged themselves to justice. The great world religions, by embracing justice and peace, all point beyond themselves to the Beloved Community, and the behavior of these clergy constituted a betrayal of their deepest religious commitments. When King writes to these clergy and names himself as one of them, he is asking them to reconsider behavior that erected a false barrier between them and him; he is asking them to be reconciled with him and, through him, with the people he represents, their Black fellow citizens.

One of the most intriguing and instructive parts of the letter has to do with a nonviolent strategy of "raising the tension." Raising the tension is the opposite of "can't we just get along" or an appeal based on the idea that we are all people of good will. Instead, the nonviolent practice of raising the tension seeks to make people uncomfortable, to prod them out of their easy, comforting ways. To raise the tension is to put matters into stark relief. Raising the tension is acting like a horsefly, inflicting painful bites in order to wake the somnolent animal up. King credits the Greek philosopher Socrates both with the tactic of raising the tension and the vivid metaphor of being a pesky gadfly.

In Plato's *Apology of Socrates*, Socrates is defending himself before a jury composed of Athenian citizens (all men), chosen by lot, in a trial for his life. We might expect the philosopher, if we didn't know him better, to throw himself on the good graces of his peers, men he knows well, but he does not. Instead, Socrates is deliberately insolent and boldly critical. He is, he tells them, their last best chance at being a better society. He compares Athens to a lazy horse and says that he is the horsefly appointed—by the gods!—to afflict them into wakefulness:

> *Now therefore, my fellow Athenians, far from making a defense on my own behalf, as one might suppose, I must make it on your behalf to prevent you from making a mistake regarding the gift the god has given you, by condemning me. For if you put me to death, you won't easily find another like me, literally, even if it's rather comical to say so, attached by the god to the city as if to a horse that, while it's large and of good stock, nevertheless is rather sluggish because of its size and needing waking up by some horse-fly, just as such, it seems to me, the god has attached me to the city—the kind of person who wakes you up, prevails upon you and reproaches each one of you and never stops landing on you all day long all over the place.[10]*

In his letter, King makes reference to that passage from Plato:

> *I just referred to the creation of tension as a part of the work of the nonviolent resister. This may sound rather shocking. But I must confess that I am not afraid of the word tension. I have earnestly worked and preached against violent tension, but there is a type of constructive nonviolent tension that is necessary for growth. Just as Socrates felt that is was necessary to create a tension in the mind so that individuals could rise from the bondage of myths and half-truths to the unfettered realm of creative analysis and objective appraisal, we must see the need of having nonviolent gadflies to create the kind of tension in society that will men to rise from the dark depths of prejudice and racism to the majestic heights of understanding and brotherhood. So the purpose of the direct action is to create a situation so crisis-packed that it will inevitably open the door to negotiation.*

Direct action is the way King tells the clergymen that he and his collaborators will be raising the tension in Birmingham, but, whether the seven addressees realized it or not, he was also raising the tension among them, by means of the letter itself. Apart from his promise of direct action, King is turning up the moral heat by making the letter an open letter, not just a private communication delivered to the seven by the U.S. Postal Service.

The letter was reported on in newspapers all over the country. And with an open letter published for all to read, the spotlight is on these white clergymen: how will they respond in the face of this heightened tension? History lets us see that the letter had a deep and lasting effect on at least one of the addressees, Roman Catholic Bishop Joseph A. Durick. Positively inspired by the message of Pope John XXIII in his Vatican II messages, and now called out by King in his letter, Durick became an outspoken advocate for Black civil rights in the segregated South. Durick's reputation changed from that of a genial clergyman who had been called the "happy priest" to a late-sixties bishop whose public appearances were boycotted by conservative Catholics. Among the seven clergymen, raising the tension worked on this small, but enormously important scale, but it worked on a much larger scale to wake up the horse of the United States, when paired with direct action.

Raising the tension was only one step in a sophisticated and methodical process of planning a nonviolent action, and King outlines the steps in the letter. One step—or practice—deserves special attention, because it creates a link with Thich Nhat Hanh's teaching of mindfulness. Along with raising the tension, King stresses one other part of the process of planning a nonviolent action: self-purification.

Self-purification is an inner, individual process, but practiced in community, not unlike the process of mindfulness in a meditating community. What self-purification means is a rigorous self-examination to determine what one's true motives are in undertaking a nonviolent direct action. One asks oneself pointedly, "Are my motives nonviolent?" King describes self-purification in the letter:

> *In any nonviolent campaign there are four basic steps: (1) Collection of the facts to determine whether injustices are alive. (2) Negotiation. (3) Self-purification and (4) Direct Action. We have gone through all of these steps in Birmingham. . . . As the weeks and months unfolded we realized that we were the victims of a broken promise. The signs remained.* Like so many experiences of the past we were confronted with blasted hopes, and the dark shadow of a deep disappointment settled upon us. So we had no alternative except that of preparing for direct action, whereby we would present our very bodies as a means of laying our case before the conscience of the local and national community. We were not unmindful of the difficulties involved. So we decided to go through a process of self-purification. We started having workshops on nonviolence and repeatedly asked ourselves the questions, "Are you able to accept blows without retaliating?" "Are you able to endure the ordeals of jail?"*

The work of civil rights advocacy and protest shows up mostly on the field of action; the letter demonstrates, through explaining self-purification, that a key part of a successful nonviolent direct action is enacted on the inner landscape of the heart and mind. King has let the addressees of the letter—and the wider American public—know that he and his companions in the cause of justice have done this work, and that the direct action is coming.

The direct action King promised was not long in coming. In the weeks that followed King's incarceration in the Birmingham jail, King and the Reverends Fred Shuttlesworth and James Bevel

---

* Racist signs placed in Birmingham stores prohibiting or sequestering Blacks away from whites.

launched the Birmingham Campaign. One part of this campaign was the Children's Crusade, in which a thousand students from local high schools, middle schools, and elementary schools left their classrooms and marched peacefully in downtown Birmingham. In response, Birmingham's commissioner of public safety, Eugene "Bull" Connor ordered the police to use force and violence to disperse the children, unleashing attack dogs on them, and using water from high-pressure hoses on them.

The "Letter from a Birmingham Jail" and the television footage of the attacks on the marching children reached a horrified American audience. The letter's powerful rhetoric was already stirring many who had read it in newspapers and magazines. Now, the direct action of the Birmingham Campaign, with its well-timed boycotts, put pressure on the local economy, and the Children's Campaign awakened the country's moral and emotional consciousness.

With the backdrop of the events of 1963, 1964 saw King receiving the highest honor for peace-loving people around the world, the Nobel Peace Prize. The on-the-ground experiences in the American South of racism and white supremacist actions worked their galvanizing effect on King; the Nobel Peace Prize lifted his vision to justice on the global scale. Beginning with his acceptance speech in Oslo on December 10, King openly accepted the responsibilities of struggles for justice all over the planet:

> After contemplation, I conclude that this award which I receive on behalf of that movement is a profound recognition that nonviolence is the answer to the crucial political and moral question of our time—the need for man to overcome oppression and violence without resorting to violence and oppression.[11]

In the same speech, King spreads out a bracing, hopeful vision that gives meaning to the very acts of terror that Blacks were experiencing in the United States, which had corollaries in countries around the world—these are birth pains of a new civilization that will be brought forth by nonviolence and love:

> *When our days become dreary with low-hovering clouds and our nights become darker than a thousand midnights, we will know that we are living in the creative turmoil of a genuine civilization struggling to be born.*

King displayed remarkable visionary insight in identifying the horror and suffering inflicted on Black Americans with the birth pangs of an authentic global community coming to be. While not named in the Nobel Peace Prize speech, it is the Beloved Community that is the "genuine civilization" that King pointed to. The Beloved Community fired King's actions and organized his thoughts. The Beloved Community was a concept that had been cherished by a series of what I call "lineage holders," each of whom worked on developing the understanding of the Beloved Community and passing it on to another. It was Howard Thurman who passed the knowledge of the Beloved Community to King.

Drew Dellinger has labeled the last years of King's life, 1966 to 1968, as the "mountaintop period." A central, defining feature of the mountaintop period is the dilation of King's consciousness, stretching toward living in the "world house." Dellinger puts it like this, enumerating six features of the mountaintop period:

> *In the last years of his life, which I call his Mountaintop Period, . . . King identified systemic links between social justice issues that were largely viewed as separate, fusing them into a unified critique that fundamentally challenged the modern system. This work articulates six aspects of King's Mountaintop Vision: (1) connecting justice*

to the cosmos, (2) emphasizing economic justice, (3) confronting systemic racism, (4) challenging U.S. militarism, (5) exemplifying the prophetic path, and (6) building a global movement.[12]

The world house that King was beginning to inhabit was the location from which King could see the Beloved Community coming to be.

The Lineage of the Beloved Community

The Beloved Community is like a third character in this biography of a friendship. The very phrase attracts and inspires. We associate the Beloved Community with towering figures like King, John Lewis, and Nhat Hanh, but they are not the only ones. Three earlier men revealed and expanded the dynamics and structure of the Beloved Community.

The lineage begins with an American philosopher, Josiah Royce, working at the end of the nineteenth century and up to the onset of World War I. At that point, a minister and union organizer, A. J. Muste, picked up what Thich Nhat Hanh called the "maintenance" of the Beloved Community, and expanded the understanding of it. From Muste, the Beloved Community was upheld by Black theologian and civil rights activist Howard Thurman. Thurman was one of King's mentors, and it is from him that King inherited the maintenance of the Beloved Community. Both Thurman and King added significantly to our understanding of the Beloved Community. Through my interviews with central figures in Thich Nhat Hanh's community in Vietnam, I learned that it was at their last meeting, at a peace conference in Geneva in 1967, that King passed his understanding of the Beloved Community to Nhat Hanh. In this chapter, the lineaments of the

Beloved Community as put forward by each of the lineage holders—Royce, Muste, Thurman, King, and Nhat Hanh—will come into view. The particular contributions of King and Nhat Hanh will receive closer attention later in the book.

I call this group of people who have maintained and helped us understand the Beloved Community "lineage holders," a term I have borrowed from schools of Buddhism. Lineage holders in Buddhism are those who have received a direct transmission of enlightenment wisdom from the previous lineage holder. There has been considerable scholarly work trying to connect King's use of the term Beloved Community and Royce. These efforts have been persuasive, but not conclusive, as they have generally centered on finding documentary evidence within the circles of academic philosophy and theology for the connection. I chose to follow another path in this work.

The year after the publication of Royce's *The Problem of Christianity* (1913), in which he introduced the Beloved Community, an international peace organization called the Fellowship of Reconciliation was founded. As Thich Nhat Hanh is in the school of Buddhism widely known as Zen, so it could be said that the Beloved Community lineage exists within the Fellowship of Reconciliation. While the concept of the Beloved Community predates the Fellowship, it was not long before influential leaders in the fellowship began further developing the concept and passing the knowledge on—that is, they became lineage holders. As in the various schools of Buddhism, the transmission of wisdom and understanding is a direct experience—so we are looking for the spark of reality, of commitment to and maintenance of the Beloved Community in tracing its lineage holders, rather than documentary evidence. Viewed in this way, as evidence of a spiritual, moral transmission from one lineage holder to another, the line of descent is clear.

Royce and the Beloved Community

Josiah Royce was born in Grass Valley, California, in 1855, one of the principal sites of the early California Gold Rush. Located in the foothills of the Sierras, Grass Valley today is a place of great beauty, with the contrast of mountains and broad valleys providing wide vistas. In the mid-nineteenth century, it must have been stunning.

Royce earned a bachelor's degree in history at the University of California at Berkeley and then a doctorate in philosophy at Johns Hopkins University. Eventually, Royce was part of the philosophy faculty at Harvard, where he worked until his death in 1916. What a journey from the Gold Rush town of Grass Valley, in a territory not yet an American state, to the highest reaches of American academia.

Looking below the surface of the bare facts of Royce's life, we find that the central feature of Royce's personality was loyalty—that he loved his family, that he stayed constant while he suffered tragedy and loss, and that he was a faithful friend. His eldest son, Christopher, began to suffer severe mental illness soon after graduating from Harvard, such that Royce and his wife later committed him to a mental institution; the young man died of typhoid in that institution at around the age of twenty-five.

A testimony to Royce's great capacity for friendship was his relationship with the eminent philosopher Charles Peirce. Peirce, because he had incurred the enmity of Harvard's president, was turned down again and again for professorships. Eventually, Peirce and his wife fell into extreme isolation and poverty. In part out of his frustration with his circumstances, he mounted increasingly polemical attacks on Royce's philosophy. Nevertheless, Royce maintained his friendship with Peirce, and even became his student in logic, through letters exchanged over a dozen years. Royce, the author of the idea of the Beloved

Community, displayed the same loyalty to friendship in his private life that he encouraged in his writing.

It was only three years before his death that Royce wrote *The Problem of Christianity*, in which he both names and describes the Beloved Community. What Royce meant by "problem" helps explain his whole rationale around the Beloved Community. In the book, Royce diagnosed the ills of his day and predicted that those ills would worsen. Christianity's problem was, as Royce saw it, how to respond positively to these societal dislocations.

When Christianity was accepted by the emperor Constantine in the fourth century, it shifted from being a persecuted, countercultural religion to being the religion of empire. Throughout the following centuries, allied with emperors and monarchs across Europe and in their colonial outposts, Christianity sought to exert a moral voice, ameliorating the worst excesses of absolutism in government—but being allied with power also corrupted Christianity. Along the way, Christianity underwent profound changes within itself, such as the Protestant Reformation, eventually breaking into many—often conflicting—denominations. Furthermore, with the anti-monarchial revolutions across Europe and the establishment of new, often secular, republics and democracies, the role of Christianity in society changed.

Such was the condition of Christianity in the early twentieth century, from Royce's vantage point. Royce also was considering what the future might hold for America and Europe. The twentieth century would bring international conflict on a new scale, beyond what had been experienced before, and with these conflicts would come technological innovations—mustard gas in WWI, the atomic bomb in WWII, and napalm in the Korean War and Vietnam. Other technological inventions and applications would spin off from these war efforts.[13]

Christianity, Royce believed, had much to offer to counter those conflicts and disruptions—love, loyalty, spiritual unity, and the "atoning conflict with evil"—but he doubted that Christianity was in a strong position to help. Deprived of its seat at the tables of power (a seat that was, in any case, corrupting and compromising), and without a single, united voice, Christianity (as well as other world religions) was impotent to lend aid when aid would be most needed.

The central idea Royce put forward in *The Problem of Christianity* is the Beloved Community itself. He described the Beloved Community not as a static object, but as an all-embracing community of all being that has not only structural shape but also a dynamic. The Beloved Community is in movement, with countless acts of loyalty or betrayal. When King used the term Beloved Community, for instance, he regularly spoke of the Beloved Community as an endpoint. Leading to the endpoint were acts of nonviolence and the work of reconciliation. For instance, in 1957, King wrote:

> *The nonviolent resister must often express his protest through noncooperation or boycotts, but noncooperation and boycotts are not ends themselves; they are merely means to awaken a sense of moral shame in the opponent. The end is redemption and reconciliation. The aftermath of nonviolence is the creation of the beloved community, while the aftermath of violence is tragic bitterness.*

And again, in 1960, highlighting the role or reconciliation:

> *There is another element that must be present in our struggle that then makes our resistance and nonviolence truly meaningful. That element is reconciliation. Our ultimate end must be the creation of the beloved community.*

The idea of an all-embracing community in flux as people either relate to it in love and loyalty or betray it all comes from

Royce's pioneering thought in *The Problem of Christianity*. In order to release the creative, healing energies that Royce believed to exist within Christianity—and to make these gifts available to society when it would need them most, a future he saw as being not far off—Royce selected a key set of New Testament ideas and translated them into terms not "owned" by religion. It is important to note that what Royce did was philosophizing, not just giving religious concepts new labels that would allow them to be adopted, unwittingly, by nonreligious people.

The idea behind the central term, Beloved Community, lives in the New Testament as the Kingdom of Heaven. What the New Testament calls "original sin" reappears as a "moral burden" and as "betrayal." "Reconciliation" is how "atonement" shows up in *The Problem of Christianity*. And love shows up in Royce's schema too. It has been well-argued that Royce was writing about a particular sort of love, translated here from the New Testament Greek as "overflowing love." Love, next to the Beloved Community itself, stands out as the most important force in the rescue system for future society that Royce bequeathed to us at the end of his life.

The root term from which Royce derived the Beloved Community is "Kingdom of Heaven." The Beloved Community is superior to an individual because though it is a person—a "live unity of knowledge and of will, of love and deed"—it is a kind of super-person whose powers are beyond those of the individual by many powers of multiplicity.[14] But why should this be? Why should a community with the characteristics of a person have such power? The answer is intimately tied to the interconnectedness of life. Not only is the Beloved Community inclusive of a diverse, multitudinous collection of people, but this population is integrated so that their gifts and potentialities are synergistic, able to accomplish more than the sum total of their energies.

Royce called Jesus of Nazareth, who preached the "nearness of the Kingdom of Heaven," "the Master." But it was to an early theologian of the church and its first systematic apologist, Paul of Tarsus—who traveled between and corresponded with a scattered group of small, nascent Christian communities—that Royce turned for many of the base concepts he used in creating the philosophic idea of the Beloved Community.

Much of what we call Paul's "theology" was based in the practical advice he gave to people trying to live in a manner worthy of the Kingdom of Heaven. For instance, in Corinth there appears to have been a division between wealthier and poorer members of the little community of believers, which manifested when they came together to share a meal and the wealthy folks did not share their plentiful (and better) food with the others. Paul warned the Corinthians that such behavior constituted a betrayal of the Kingdom of Heaven, where, in reality, "As one suffers, all suffer; if one rejoices, all rejoice." Elsewhere, Paul taught the essential unity of faithful humans in the person of Christ: "There is no longer Jew or Greek, there is no longer slave or free, there is no longer male or female; for all of you are one in Christ Jesus."[15]

That is to say—in Royce's terms—the Beloved Community is living, unified, of divine status, and has the quality of personhood:

> But it is also true that Christianity not only is a religion founded upon the idea of the divine community—the Church—but also is a religion whose human founder was rather the community itself, acting as a spiritual unity.

The Beloved Community Is Inclusive of All

For Royce, the Beloved Community transcended nations and religions; he called it inclusive of all, a spiritual unity for the whole human race.[16] The human race, if spiritually unified, matures across time. The more mature expressions of religion appear as loyalty to the universal community.[17]

Royce wrote *The Problem of Christianity* at the dawn of the twentieth century, as a professor at Harvard College. While nothing in *The Problem of Christianity* explicitly excludes women or people of color, we cannot assume that when Royce uses terms like "man" or "mankind," he means to include women and people of color, who were, after all, largely excluded from his professional world and from equal participation in society in general.

King, of course, would powerfully push the constricted boundaries of a self-avowedly all-inclusive Beloved Community to consciously and truly include Black Americans and the formal enemies of America at the time, the Vietnamese, but what of women? As Karen Guth has written,

> *What are feminists and womanists to make of Martin Luther King Jr.'s theological and political legacy? On one hand, feminists and womanists can find much to admire in his commitment to justice, his ability to identify connections between various forms of oppression, and his embrace of love as a political practice. On the other hand, despite King's leadership of one of the most important movements for equal rights in American history, he paid little attention to gender injustice. He spoke often of the "triple evils of poverty, racism, and war" but never identified sexism as an equally pernicious evil. Moreover, King struggled personally to treat female civil rights activists and other women as equals.[18]*

The inclusion of all beings in the "universal" circle of the Beloved Community would have to wait until Thich Nhat Hanh became a proponent of the Beloved Community.[19] We may think, then, of Nhat Hanh, King, and, as we shall see, Muste and Thurman perfecting each other—and Royce as well—as their insights deepen across time. Or, we might say that each lineage holder polished the lens through which we see the Beloved Community.

Original Sin and the Moral Burden

Original sin is an early Christian doctrine that Royce saw as important in the great system of dynamic forces supporting and maintaining (and betraying and breaking down) the Beloved Community. As with all the other aspects of the Beloved Community that Royce drew forth from New Testament sources, though, he transformed original sin into a philosophic concept—a "moral burden"—that he hoped would be useful for people struggling with societal ills. He focused on a common experience of modern people—the gap between their inner convictions and the external pressure to conform to the overwhelming powers of the day: economic and political, centrally, backed up by military might and law, whether just or unjust. The more aware a person becomes about the political and social realities—and about the power dynamics and structural injustices that press down upon people from all sides and at all times—the greater the gap between their personal convictions and the "world" becomes. That is, the moral burden becomes heavier and heavier the more one knows.

The gap between the inner self and the outer moral code of society becomes greater and greater, Royce says, with the increasing sophistication of both individual and society. The individual knows and understands more and more about his or her own inner life, and the overall maturation of the human race presents to the individual an ever more developed moral philosophy.

The individual can be absolved neither of the "inherited" guilt into which he or she is born nor of the particular offenses that the individual might commit. It is by resorting to another level—the level of the spiritually united, all-inclusive community—that reconciliation can be effected.[20]

Loyalty

As the individual and the entirety of humanity become more spiritually mature, it becomes easier to glimpse the Beloved Community. Here is where the description of the universal community as "beloved" begins to have meaning. The universal community becomes the object of the greatest love, and the virtue of loyalty is awakened with respect to this great community. In fact, it is the universal community that is the actor, eliciting loyalty to itself from the individual.[21]

Loyalty, for Royce, is connected to grace, the healing and restoring energies that flow from the level of the infinite or universal to the individual. When a person or a community experiences grace, the condition has been set for activating loyalty to the source of grace. If grace is experienced within the container of the faith community, it is easy to see that those who benefit from grace will give the community their loving loyalty.

Linking loyalty, however, to love for the Beloved Community creates a heightened peril with respect to the moral burden. Returning to the conflict within the Corinthian community over the distribution of food in communal dinners, Paul writes,

> *Whoever, therefore, eats the bread or drinks the cup of the Lord in an unworthy manner will be answerable for the body and blood of the Lord. Examine yourselves, and only then eat of the bread and drink of the cup. For all who eat and drink without discerning the body [some ancient authorities add, "of the Lord"], eat and drink judgment against themselves.*[22]

Though it is difficult to get a clear picture of what the gathering Paul calls "the Lord's supper" looks like in detail, we can see that Paul develops a coherent view of the universal Christian community as an interconnected body, bound together by the energy of love. This body is equal to the resurrected Christ and is worthy, thus, of the Christian's own love and loyalty. To have once, in baptism, made vows of loyalty to Christ as the body of the universal church, and then to betray those promises of loving loyalty, is to bring on oneself and the local community dire consequences: "For this reason many of you are weak and ill, and some of you have died."[23]

A striking feature of loyalty as Royce has it is that as our loyalties expand, moving toward the Beloved Community, we do not drop our "lesser" loyalties. Both King and Nhat Hanh exemplify this aspect of the Roycean Beloved Community. The late civil rights activist Dr. Vincent Harding—who wrote the first draft of King's landmark speech at Riverside Church, "Beyond Vietnam"—claimed that King faced criticism and opposition from supporters and allies as he expanded his commitments to include peace in Vietnam, international economic justice, and domestic poverty. They feared he was letting go of his civil rights activism—that his loyalty to the fight for civil rights for Black Americans would be weakened or diluted in the process. For King, however, the idea of abandoning his expanded loyalty to international issues would amount to a betrayal of the Beloved Community.

Atonement/Reconciliation

Betrayal of the vows—the expressions of loyalty—to the Beloved Community is sin under the general heading of the moral burden. In Christian theology, atonement is the remedy for sin; for Royce, atonement (reconciliation) is needed to heal the betrayal of the Kingdom of Heaven (Beloved Community).

Treason and betrayal have particular meanings within the Beloved Community. Betrayal of another individual is not betrayal of the Beloved Community, unless the one who is betrayed is betrayed precisely because of their association with the Beloved

Community. Treason initiates a deep sort of rupture within the community, one that cannot be repaired through ordinary civility or even friendship. Rather, to be overcome, treason needs an avatar of the Beloved Community who will undertake a "creative act of love" to bring about reconciliation. This servant of reconciliation must, of course, be loyal to the Beloved Community in their own person.[24]

Royce goes on to specify that the "creative act of love" to be performed by the avatar of the community needs to link to the act of treason, to somehow be shaped by this act of treason—reconciliation is earthy, practical, and confronts the betrayal in direct terms.[25] This is reminiscent of Nhat Hanh's insistence that the manifestation of nirvana is practical and this-worldly, not abstract and present only in a supernal realm. Looking forward, Royce's insistence on an atoning act being genuinely responsive to the betrayal itself is expressed in King's and his movement partners' plans for each nonviolent action being fully cognizant of the local conditions and history.

In one of Royce's most hopeful statements, he says that the world that lies on the other side of the work of reconciliation is not only better because the brokenness—the treason—has been addressed, but also is better than it was before the treason occurred.[26] In the same way, if a person hurts a friend, realizes their mistake, and then comes to a true reconciliation with the friend, their friendship can be stronger and deeper than it was before the harm was done. In accordance with his idea of a world that is maturing spiritually, Royce envisions a world moving toward a more complete and integrated state. The church of the New Testament, Spirit-filled, is an advance upon the unenlightened pre-Resurrection community of Jesus's followers, and this New Testament narrative arc is behind Royce's hope-filled expectations about the post-reconciliation community.[27]

Love

Love is the last element in the Roycean version of the Beloved Community. The word *love* appears hundreds of times in *The Problem of Christianity*. One scholar, Gary Herstein, argues that while *agape* love—a type of love that is often translated as "unconditional" or "sacrificial" love (I usually translate agape as "overflowing love")—per se does not show up in Royce's *Problem of Christianity*, it is undeniably present under the guise of loyalty.[28] Another scholar proposes that for Royce, adding sacrifice to loyalty makes an amalgam that is, in total, agape love, and that this love is the ordering principle of the Beloved Community:

> For Royce, the "beloved community" was the ideal Christian community, which is founded upon loyalty and sacrifice. . . . Although King's conception of the "beloved community" epresents a synthesis from a wide range of thinkers, a simple working definition is "a community ordered by love." . . . Love refers to the Christian conception of "agape."[29]

Linking loyalty and sacrifice to produce agape is convincing, but it needs careful distinction not to be misleading. Royce takes pains to say that Christian love is not self-abnegation but is "heroic." But how can sacrifice not lead to ideas of self-abnegation? Royce says that God's love for the individual is the pouring of the infinite into the finite—we are full of God's love. Our sacrifice is from an overflow of love within us that comes from God, not our own human love.[30] The goal of the Christian is first to rejoice in God's love and then to awaken the neighbor to the fact that he or she is equally loved, so that the neighbor too becomes a lover, spreading love to others.[31]

Royce's reading of love in the New Testament conforms to his view that Jesus taught ethics and spirituality for individuals and that it remained for Paul to teach loyalty, love, sacrifice, and the work of reconciliation, with the universal community as the ultimate object of attention. For instance, Jesus taught love of neighbor as self, while Paul taught communities of Christians to love and provide for the whole church.

Looking forward to King, it is easy to see that his understanding of love has this positive, sourced-in-the-infinite quality. Royce also helps us see agape as what he calls "heroic," an action from strength, God's strength, rather than a kind of passivity and, in Royce's term, self-abnegation. I remember that in Middleburg, Virginia, where I pastored a small Episcopal congregation, one of my parishioners said that King's 1963 book *Strength to Love*, a collection of sermons, had changed his life and given him the strength to love. A central contribution by King is clearly identifying the love that glues the Beloved Community together as "overflowing love," agape love.

The Roycean Beloved Community on the Eve of World War I

Royce wrote one more book that had the Beloved Community as its central topic, *The Hope of the Great Community*, published in 1916, at the very end of his life. For Royce, nonviolence is not one of the virtues of the Beloved Community. This passage from *The Hope of the Great Community* illustrates his attitude well:

> Such converts to the doctrine that war is good ascribe their sudden conversion to the wonder and reverence which have been aroused in them by the sight of France re-generated through the very dangers which the invader has brought with him, awakened to a new sense that the value of life lies not in what individuals get out of it, but in what the exertions and the perils of war call out and illustrate, namely, the supreme and super-individual value of loyalty. Loyalty, the devotion of the self to the interests of the community, is indeed the form which the highest life of humanity must

take, whether in a political unity, such as in a nation, or in the church universal, such as Paul foresaw. Without loyalty, there is no salvation.[32]

The Beloved Community as Royce outlined it included three central elements—the Beloved Community, moral burden, and atonement. To these central three, he added loyalty and love (and, nested within moral burden, treason toward the Beloved Community). That Royce valorized war and presented it as consonant with the values of the Beloved Community is not surprising from the vantage of the history of Western peace movements in the twentieth century. Becoming a conscientious objector in the United States during World War I, for example, required undergoing a medical exam. If the applicant passed the exam, the next stop was an army camp where intense coercion was applied, with the majority of applicants finally caving in and becoming combatants. Withering public censure met the successful applicant for conscientious objector status.[33] Peace and nonviolence became ideals of the Beloved Community later, through the Fellowship of Reconciliation—additions which had tremendous transformative power, not least in the momentous outcomes they led to through the American civil rights movement with King.

The Fellowship of Reconciliation

The Fellowship of Reconciliation (FoR) was founded in England in 1914, at a peace conference held at Cambridge University. A second branch of FoR was founded in the United States a year later. Both King and Nhat Hanh were members, and it was FoR that brought King and Nhat Hanh together for their first meeting in Chicago, in 1966, a meeting arranged by long-time FoR leader A. J. Muste. It is almost undoubtedly true that FoR, perhaps in the person of Muste, carried forward the lineage of the

Beloved Community, and from FoR King received the lineage. The actual lines of transmission are murky:* the founders of FoR in the United States were a group of about seventy pacifists—and a pacifist, as we have seen, Royce was not. A thorough history of FoR in the United States by Paul Dekar, a former FoR president, contains Beloved Community in the title but is silent on Royce's connection with FoR.[34]

FoR began first in England, at a peace conference at Cambridge University in 1914.[35] At that time, pacifism was not only a minority position, even in the churches, but one that could entail personal danger. Several of the early FoR members in England were put under death sentences, though the sentences were commuted.[36]

A good illustration of how against the tide the FoR pacifist stance was during this era can be found in William Temple, an English aristocrat and cleric, son of an archbishop of Canterbury and himself to become the Archbishop of Canterbury, helping guide the nation and the Christian world through the second World War. The young William Temple (33 at the time) attended a Cambridge meeting in September 1914, shortly before the larger gathering that established FoR.[37] While Temple is remembered for his internationalism and efforts to begin the healing of the rifts between European nations during his tenure as Archbishop of Canterbury, he would not associate formally with FoR and publicly supported England's involvement in World War I.

---

* To illustrate the blurred understanding of the relationship of Royce to the Fellowship of Reconciliation, an internet search found multiple sites that claimed unequivocally that Royce was the founder of FOR, some adding that he founded the organization in 1913, two years before FoR came to the United States.

The United States Fellowship of Reconciliation was established in 1915, one year after the Cambridge meeting. One of the FoR founders and leaders in England, Henry Hodgkin, visited the fledgling American FoR as it was being organized in 1915, and had this skeptical comment:

> *A meeting in this country [America] is sure to get onto somewhat different lines from ours. The American turn of mind seems to demand more in the way of immediate expression in act, perhaps in corporate act, and the situation here has not that element of extreme difficulty which has made us so careful in taking any step. This has, I see, been our strength, for it has driven us back on fundamentals, and it has caused us to think all round our position before rushing into action. I don't see how people here can hold themselves in from "doing something" very soon after they are organized.[38]*

Hodgkin's comment, meant to be derogatory, is paradoxically prescient, as the FoR influence on King and other civil rights and peace activists certainly contributed to historic "corporate acts" that have both changed the United States, and the world. Hodgkin was also wrong about a strong differential in the costs for adherence to pacifism between the United States and England—pacificism would prove to be costly in both countries. In my own denomination, the Episcopal Church, Bishop Paul Jones was censured by a committee of the House of Bishops and eventually resigned his seat. A founding member of FoR and the missionary bishop of Utah, Bishop Jones paid a high price for being a pacifist in the United States—he never held a permanent post as bishop again.

Pacifism, as held by the early FoR, was not the nonviolence of King. There is a long journey between 1915 and King's embrace and reshaping of the Beloved Community in the late 1950s and early 1960s. It is to that journey that we turn now.

A. J. Muste, the Fellowship of Reconciliation, and the Evolution to Nonviolent Resistance

A. J. Muste was an early member of the Fellowship of Reconciliation and later its director. He wrote prolifically on nonviolence throughout the first half of the twentieth century. Muste's influence on and contributions to the nonviolent movement were monumental and led to him being once called "one of the towering pillars of the twentieth century."[39] His importance is best summed up in a telegram Martin Luther King Jr. sent to Muste on his eightieth birthday in February 1965:

> *You have climbed the mountain and have seen the great and abiding truth to which you have dedicated your life. Throughout the world you are honored as our most effective exponent of pacifism. You have been a great friend and inspiration to me and the whole nonviolent movement. Without you the American Negro might never have caught the meaning of true love for humanity.*[40]

Muste also made important contributions to the concept of the Beloved Community. Under his influence, pacifism becomes nonviolent resistance, and Muste affirms that a personal God is the originator of the nonviolent path—nonviolence is in accord with the normative shape of the universe's energy. Finally, Muste asserts that the practitioner of nonviolence must be prepared to sacrifice their life for the cause of justice and that the result of such a sacrifice is the release of divine energy into the sphere of human activity.

For the most part, pacifist movements in the early twentieth century did not contain the element of resistance. While there were others besides Muste who were developing a more active form of pacifism, Muste's and leadership in the sixteen-week-long strike of textile workers in Lawrence, Massachusetts in 1912, three years before the formation of the Fellowship of

Reconciliation, catapulted him into prominence in the nonviolent resistance movement.[41] The shift of FoR and, in general, the move from pacifism per se to nonviolent resistance was neither smooth nor without argument. Giants in the religious world and in civil society in general, such as Reinhold Niebuhr, who was for a time director of FoR, held that nonviolent resistance was not nonviolent at all and eschewed the development.* Both Muste's long-time commitment to nonviolent resistance and his insistence for a willingness for self-sacrifice helped overcome opposition within FoR and usher in an embrace of nonviolent resistance.

In Royce's transmutation of explicitly Christian categories into his enunciation of the Beloved Community, the idea of martyrdom and self-sacrifice is broadened to a "creative act of love."[42] Muste seems to constrict Royce's more expansive concept, pulling back into a "true crucifixion":

> *If the ultimate expression of violence is killing the opponent, the "aggressor," the ultimate expression of nonviolence or soul force is quite as obviously the willingness and ability to die at the hands and on behalf of the evildoer. The pacifist must be ready to pay that price. . . . The suffering need not be sought. Indeed it must not be. Martyrdom for the sake of martyrdom is suicide by exhibitionism, not redemptive crucifixion. But we may not seek to evade suffering. It must be voluntarily accepted. The model for accepting such sacrifice is passion and death. . . . Then God has entered into history and its course has been forever changed. Here is released the power which in the political and social realm is the counterpart of the*

---

* We will see, when King inherits and begins to work with the Beloved Community Complex, that he will struggle with his high regard for Niebuhr on the one hand, and with his growing sense of the rightness of nonviolent resistance on the other.

fission of the atom and the release of atomic energy in its realm. If the Christian religion means anything, it means this. If the experience of mankind has taught anything, it teaches this.[43]

Muste's passionate expression of the pacifist's willingness to accept "crucifixion" for the cause of justice may well have impressed critics with the seriousness of the pacifist position. And by linking the active pacifist's position with the sacrifice of Christ on the cross, Muste made a bold assertion: the cause of the nonviolent resister is identified with the ministry and mission of Jesus Christ. And by implication, Muste rooted the path of nonviolent opposition in the nature of a just God and thus into the warp and weft of the universe God created and sustains—a potent claim in the Christian world.

At the same time, Muste may have reawakened an ancient Christian debate that calls into question any witness to peace and justice that does not end in bloodshed, that is, the willingness to persevere to the point of execution for the cause. He may have unwittingly restricted the creativity of peaceful witness that could encompass both a Martin Luther King Jr. and a Thich Nhat Hanh. In other words, while Muste's memorable language about the willingness to sacrifice one's life may have helped normalize the pacifist position in the first half of the twentieth century, he may also have set up an implication that only "blood sacrifice" is related to the release of divine healing energies.

The original meaning of the word *martyr* is simply "witness." Like King and those who self-immolated in Vietnam, fidelity to the truth and to justice may, ultimately, demand the sacrifice of one's life. For others, however, like Nhat Hanh, the status of unwavering witness, martyrdom in its fundamental sense, is undoubted. Language like that of Muste may have had the unintended effect of obscuring the role of martyrs who testify with their lived lives rather than by their deaths.

Further, as can be seen in the previous quotation, Muste defines the boundaries of atoning sacrifice as being only those deaths that are not sought out but are the unintended results of the encounter between the nonviolent activist and violent exponents of an unjust system. In the future, this would set up a struggle for King, who admired Muste, when he is confronted with Nhat Hanh's justification of the self-immolation of Buddhists in Vietnam. Should these Buddhists be regarded as martyrs, in the same league with martyrs in the American civil rights movement whose suffering and death are imposed upon them from the outside?

Muste promoted an engaged pacifism, secular in character; almost paradoxically he appealed to a personal God as the source of his nonviolent action; and he moved beyond the confines of the church to be active with protestors of all stripes of religious commitment, as well as with those who were avowedly areligious or even opposed to religion. All of that, along with his personal integrity and long-term witness, shaped and forwarded the Beloved Community lineage in significant ways. His leadership of the nonviolent resistance movement stretched from the early twentieth century well into the protests against the Vietnam War. And while Muste supported the Civil Rights movement, it fell to another FoR leader, Howard Thurman, to extend the FoR vision to race relations within the United States.

Howard Thurman, Race, and the Beloved Community

Like Muste, Thurman was a prominent member of the Fellowship of Reconciliation. A Black man fourteen years Muste's junior, it was Thurman who turned the attention of the fellowship to racial reconciliation. It is illustrative to see how these two formative leaders in the fellowship, Muste and Thurman, reacted to Walter Rauschenbusch, a profoundly influential social theologian of the time. For Muste, a white man, Rauschenbusch seems to have been an uncomplicated mentor.

By contrast, when Thurman met the famous Rauschenbusch, he was struck by the high-minded disregard Rauschenbusch displayed toward questions of racial justice. Thurman learned positive and negative lessons from Rauschenbusch. The deeply searching Thurman came to the conclusion that international and domestic peace and justice efforts that pretended that race in the United States was not a limiting and self-defeating factor were seriously flawed, and he critiqued Rauschenbusch's position. Thurman took the work of nonviolent activism within the Fellowship of Reconciliation into the heart of American society in the area of racial justice and reconciliation.

It is also significant that it was Thurman who was first in a chain of great Black civil rights thinkers and activists to journey to India to meet with Mohandas K. Gandhi (or, after Gandhi's death, to learn from those carrying on his movement for *swaraj* (self-rule achieved through nonviolent protest).The core of Gandhi's teaching, a principle absorbed by Black civil rights activists who learned from Gandhi and his movement is contained in the term *satyagraha*, a neologism coined by Gandhi. Often translated as "soul force," satyagraha claims a transforming power for nonviolent social change. The practice of satyagraha is consciously and willingly taking on the burden of social injustice while resolutely holding to one's principles and maintaining a nonviolent stance. Gandhi and his followers believed that the witness provided by the practice of satyagraha converts the unjust oppressor without resorting to violence in kind. Satyagraha became a guiding principle in the Fellowship of Reconciliation from Thurman on. After Thurman, two other leading Black ministers—Benjamin Mays and Mordecai Johnson—made their own pilgrimages to India. Mays and Johnson, each in his own way, were important models for King. King himself made this pilgrimage twenty-three years after Thurman, a journey that reinforced the lessons of active nonviolence he had already begun imbibing.

Thurman's great contributions to the Beloved Community may be said to be capped by the adding of racial reconciliation and civil rights to the focus of the Fellowship and to the understanding of the Beloved Community. But there were also other important contributions. His journey to India and meeting with Gandhi added a new, robust theoretical foundation for peace activism, summed up in the term introduced previously, satyagraha. Gandhi was an activist, yes, but a theorist as well, and his thoughts on pacifism were published in the *Fellowship* numbers of times.[*] In addition, the living example of an oppressed people—people of color—successfully throwing off the rule of the British using satyagraha was a bracing and inspiring lesson for Thurman and one that he carried back to the United States. Nonviolent resistance in India gave new energy to the race struggles in the United States.

As Muste was granted, as he saw it, visionary affirmations from God on his path of nonviolent activism, so was Thurman bolstered by his experience of the limitless power of the divine as the sublime. While Muste's mystic affirmations were cruciform in character—that is, patterned by the central theology of the life, death, and resurrection of Jesus as the Christ of God—for Thurman, there were foundational experiences of the power and numinosity of the divine in nature, experiences that stretched back to his childhood in coastal Florida. There the

---

[*] In addition to the influences of Muste and Thurman, Glenn Smiley and Bayard Rustin—both FoR members—worked closely with King to bring the philosophy and practice of Gandhian active nonviolence into the American civil rights movement.

young Thurman was drawn outside to witness the overwhelming power of gathering hurricanes, power that he identified not with a mindless force of destruction, but with the infinite power of God.

The shape and content of Thurman's mystic experiences influenced the direction he took the Fellowship of Reconciliation, just as Muste's cruciform experiences of the divine shaped his. In Thurman's case, what might be termed "nature mysticism" prepared Thurman to receive sympathetically the religious witness of people far from his credal base in American Protestantism. Beyond differences in their respective mystic experiences, with Muste and Thurman there emerges a trend in the development of the Beloved Community—the influence of religious experience in what may seem a rational, theological, or philosophical development. Muste, Thurman, King, and Nhat Hanh all recorded pivotal experiences that can be understood as the emotional, intellectual, spiritual, or physical response to great forces from beyond them. The mystic experiences of Thurman's are in keeping with Royce's stipulating that the Beloved Community is of divine origin and that the divine acts upon both the community and the individual.

As we seek to understand the friendship of King and Nhat Hanh and to understand the third party in this biography, the Beloved Community itself, we have to face the reality that the lineage holders of the Beloved Community are religious people. It is equally important, however, to see that no one religion owns the Beloved Community. When Royce unhooked the Beloved Community and its concepts from its New Testament setting, he simultaneously took the concepts out of the hands of Christian theologians and began an evolution of the understanding of the Beloved Community that went further than he may have envisioned.

Given Royce's concern that the Beloved Community serve the changing and expanding needs of human society, it is not hard to believe that Royce would welcome the freedom, the changing play of ideas about the Beloved Community that have come in the decades since he wrote *The Problem of Christianity*.

Later, when we turn to Nhat Hanh's contributions to understanding the Beloved Community, we will witness the extraordinary gesture he makes in releasing the leadership of the Beloved Community into our hands. He encourages an understanding of it that goes beyond not only Christianity but also Buddhism. The Beloved Community may still be thought of as being of divine origin, of being related to the sacred, but no creed or dogma will be able to hold it within its confines.

But of what consequence is it that the Beloved Community is of divine origin? Does it matter? For Royce and lineage holders who followed him, the divine origin of the Beloved Community was an essential element in what Nhat Hanh called the "maintaining" of the Beloved Community. To maintain the Beloved Community is to recognize that the Beloved Community can be betrayed, and that in the aftermath of betrayal, we must act to restore, repair, and heal.

For both King and Nhat Hanh, love acts in the universe to heal and to transform when there has been betrayal and injury. According to the New Testament sources Royce drew upon when he was defining the Beloved Community, love is of God and is even equated with God. Here is a beautiful statement by Nhat Hanh that could easily be thought to have come from one of the New Testament writings about divine love:

> *I don't know what tomorrow will bring, but no matter what happens, I don't think my friends will be robbed of their faith. Our faith is not built on shaky ground or esoteric understanding. It is faith in the strength of unconditional love. It asks nothing in*

return and cannot be shaken even by betrayal.... This love arises from the individual psyche, and yet the gradual eroding or sudden destruction of that psyche cannot diminish this love. It is a transcendent, ultimate love. Ordinary love can go up in smoke when confronted by your lover's faults or betrayal. Transcendent love can never diminish. . . .

For Nhat Hanh, then, a love that is both here and now, present in our lives and at the same time coursing through the universe, helps us as we meet betrayal and disappointment in our lives. For King, this same transcendent love had the qualities of a person, and so he could appeal to divine love—he could pray. In the early 1960s King wrote:

*In the past the idea of a personal God was little more than a metaphysical category that I found theologically and philosophically satisfying. Now it is a living reality that has been validated in the experiences of everyday life. God has been profoundly real to me in recent years. . . . So in the truest sense of the Word, God is a living God. In him there is feeling and will, responsive to the deepest yearnings of the human heart; **this** God both evokes and answers prayer.*

One of King's most quoted statements is this: "The arc of the moral universe is long but it bends toward justice." If we sit with this famous statement a while, some questions might arise: Is the moral universe the highest values we share as humans? Or does the world have not only consciousness but also a moral code that lives within it?

The idea of a moral universe connects with a universe that pulses with overflowing, unconditional love, divine love. Such an idea is not without troubling aspects, such as, who "speaks" for the universe? For thousands of years, people with great power have justified their domination by claiming a divine mandate. Keeping in mind the problem of facile claims about knowing the mind of God, or saying our position is ordained by God, we might still believe that the Beloved Community is not only an end, but also a dynamic process, love in action, maintaining and manifesting itself through the loving actions of those loyal to it.

The caution is to prevent our imputing, projecting upon the idea of the divine qualities and values that are convenient for human ends. What countless memoirs and personal narratives through the ages attest to, however, is that divine love—love literally overflowing some boundary between the unseen and the sensible—comes to us, surprising us. We often call this experience "grace." Quite the opposite of projection upon the divine, grace is the gift of a cosmos to us, its grateful recipients.

King and the Beloved Community

King was the great synthesizer of the understanding of the Beloved Community. He is the lineage holder who brought the Beloved Community into the consciousness of the world. And, he is the one who made it "operational," who maintained the Beloved Community through the strategies of nonviolent protest.

King melded the pacifism he received from Muste and others in the Fellowship of Reconciliation with the Gandhian concepts of nonviolence. King contributed an article to the September 1958 issue of *Fellowship*, "My Pilgrimage to Nonviolence." In this article, King's voice is not that of the preacher or the prophet, but that of a scholar. King tells us that it was a lecture by A. J. Muste at Crozer Seminary that introduced him to the "pacifist position."[44]

Like Muste and Thurman before him, King read Rauschenbusch and found that his *Christianity and the Social Crisis* left an "indelible imprint on [his] thinking."[45] Acknowledging the contributions of Rauschenbusch, he also levels a critique at him, faulting Rauschenbusch for too closely identifying "the Kingdom of God with a particular social and economic system—a tendency that should never befall the Church."[46]

King next shares his critique of both Marxism and capitalism, two of the great social systems of the twentieth century.[47] From there, he describes his first encounter with another great social system, Gandhism, in a 1949 lecture by Dr. Mordecai Johnson, the president of Howard University.[48] Whereas King criticizes his other intellectual interlocuters in this *Fellowship* article, he is wholly approving of what he learned about Gandhi's nonviolence.

In reviewing Royce and the origin of the concept of the Beloved Community, I noted Royce did not name the love that is the organizing, dynamic principle of the Beloved Community as agape; rather, this was done by King as a lineage holder. King returned to the same New Testament sources used by Royce and spotlighted a particular kind of love that sounds its notes like a flute line in Afro-Cuban jazz, elevating and lightening the whole piece. It is not the love of coworkers, respecting each other, working companionably side by side; it is not the love of Eros—one of the first of the Greek gods, who sprang into being at the beginning of creation*—a love that desires the beloved to the point of being consumed; and it is not the love of friendship, which is an enduring, ripening love that can last a lifetime. Rather, the love of the Beloved Community is agape—unconditional, sacrificial, overflowing love.

King also reexamined the idea of interconnection, which, like love, was present from the onset in Royce's formulation of the Beloved Community. King's passages in his sermons and speeches on the "interrelated structure of reality" seem at first to be somewhat repetitive. Closer examination, however, reveals

---

* Hesiod places Eros among the earliest of the gods; Plato, in the *Symposium*, names Eros as the first of the gods.

that in the mountaintop period, King's understanding of the Beloved Community and interrelatedness grew. In 1965 it seems that he saw the Christian church as interconnected, member to member. But by the end of his life, King was consciously living as a world citizen in what he called the world house. King didn't reach so far as Nhat Hanh with the realization that all people and all of life are part of the Beloved Community, but he advanced a more life-embracing vision of the Beloved Community than did Royce, Muste, and Thurman.

King details his changeable relationship with the thought of Reinhold Niebuhr, who, after having served as a director of FoR, broke with the organization over active nonviolence. King records his growing dissatisfaction with Niebuhr's arguments against pacifism, and he moves to a firmer embrace of pacifism after a thorough analysis of Niebuhr's positions.[49]

King concludes his description of his "pilgrimage" with a brief account of his doctoral studies at Boston University. There, King's belief in a personal God of love—bolstered, as has been said, by spiritual experiences—found philosophical grounding in personalism, as taught by Edgar S. Brightman and L. Harold DeWolf. Ultimately, however, it was his experience of the Montgomery Bus Boycott that united his studied positions on nonviolence with the teachings of Jesus and of Gandhi. "Many of the things that I had not cleared up intellectually concerning nonviolence were now solved in the sphere of practical action."[50]

African American Christianity, personalistic theology and philosophy, Gandhian nonviolence, European and American labor organizing strategies, and the tactics of pacifism—King mixed all of these and turned out a powerful amalgam that he then successfully enacted in mass movements, boycotts, and strikes—leading the American people in "'doing something' . . . after they are organized."

Behind King's operational genius we can see a rare mind at work, that of the synthesizer. Most scholars focus on one field. Far rarer are scholars who weave together strands from different disciplines. It is often from such weaving that a new paradigm, a truer picture of reality, emerges. King was such a synthesizer. Rarest of all, however, is the scholar who can move from the realm of the theoretical into activism, as King did.

A Letter across the Divide

I t is important to first understand the significant barriers—religious, political, and social—that lay between Thich Nhat Hanh and Martin Luther King Jr., before we can understand how the successful bridging of this gap highlights the precious quality of their friendship. From today's standpoint, these barriers might not appear formidable, but this is almost certainly, in part, due to the efforts of King and Nhat Hanh, along with many others, that changed the social and religious conditions in the United States such that friendships like theirs might flourish more easily. In the 1950s and '60s, friendships across barriers of race and religion were not only uncommon but could prove dangerous.

For instance, consider the experience of Opel Lee, the nonagenarian advocate for making Juneteenth a Federal holiday. Lee's parents moved with their young daughter into a white neighborhood of Fort Worth, Texas, in 1939. The realtors who sold Lee's parents their new home told them that they would encounter no problem with their white neighbors. Instead, within a week and on the occasion of Juneteenth, a mob estimated at 500 people surrounded the house, invaded it, dragged the furniture into the street and set the Lee's possessions ablaze. And even though the efforts of King, Nhat Hanh and many others have improved race and religious respect in the United States, the instances in the twenty-first century of anti-Muslim violence and violence against Asians yields current testimony to the enduring power of prejudice.

By no means was Buddhism a new topic and presence in the United States by the middle of the twentieth century. D. T. Suzuki and Soyen Shaku, for example, helped to spread a version of Zen in America throughout the first half of the twentieth century. Suzuki especially promoted an experience and practice-based version of Zen that appealed to qualities that resonated with American ideals: a "no nonsense," accessible religion that was often called no religion at all, but a philosophy of life. The practice of Zen required determination, not adherence to creeds and dogma. Zen Buddhism accorded with William James's emphasis on religious experience, not doctrine, as the fount of subsequent tradition. The Beats picked up on Zen, partly through the influence of California poet Gary Snyder, a sponsorship that brought it into popular culture.

Despite this, American exposure to Buddhism was still comparatively fresh. The eloquent Alan Watts gave his popular lectures on Zen and other Buddhist and Hindu themes on the Berkeley radio station KPFA from 1953 to 1962. Watt's widely-read book *The Way of Zen* was published in 1957. Shunryu Suzuki founded the San Francisco Zen Center in 1962, but it wasn't until 1969 that he established Tassajara Zen Mountain Center, in Big Sur, California, one of the first Buddhist training monasteries outside of Asia. His popular book *Zen Mind, Beginner's Mind* was not published until 1970.

Likewise, Tibetan Buddhism, and particularly the Vajrayana form of Buddhism, made its spectacular entrance into the United States with Chögyam Trungpa Rinpoche only in 1970. Institutions that Chögyam Trungpa Rinpoche founded—such as his Shambhala meditation centers, Naropa University, and Shambhala Publications—helped spread awareness about Tibetan Buddhism around the United States and the world.

Seven years later, in 1977, Harvey Cox, a Professor of Divinity at Harvard University, would write *Turning East*, a retrospective survey of the influx and influence of Asian religions in the United States. Cox's book has the feel of freshness about it; he is not peering far back in time but is taking a look at the contemporary religious landscape in the United States of the late seventies and some of the preceding decades.* In summary, while Buddhism was present in the cultural conversation of the 1960s, the coming together in friendship of a Buddhist and a Christian at this time was not a commonplace encounter.

In addition to the relative newness of Buddhism in popular culture, the war raging between the United States and Vietnam could only make the Nhat Hanh/King friendship more unlikely and potentially fraught. Several sources date the flowering of the anti–Vietnam War movement in the United States to 1965.

Finally, their social positions: Nhat Hanh was celibate, a monk from the age of sixteen; King was married and a minister. Monasticism, while holding a prominent position in the two largest Christian bodies—Roman Catholicism and Easter Orthodoxy—is decidedly a minority presence in Protestant Christianity, and entirely absent from the most reformed bodies, such as the Baptist Church. The life of Nhat Hanh would have been foreign and exotic to most Protestants.

Thich Nhat Hanh's poem, "Our Green Garden" was published in the *New York Review of Books* on June 9, 1966, just days after he

---

* I would be remiss not to acknowledge the hugely influential work of Alan Watts in making accessible and popularizing Asian religious thought and practice. Watts was both a professor and administrator of the American Academy of Asian Studies in San Francisco, an institution that has a lineal relationship to my institution, the California Institute of Integral Studies. Watts's major publications somewhat predate the wave of Asian religion and philosophy in the United States to which I've gestured in this section.

and King held their joint press conference in Chicago regarding the war. Thus, as their friendship begins, it is founded on the grounds of a war protest that was only starting to gain cultural traction. Nhat Hanh and King must have summoned thought and courage to cross the barriers of culture, race, politics, and religion to hold this press conference together. Sitting beside one another behind the phalanx of microphones that broadcast their voices, Nhat Hanh and King were the embodiment of interconnected reality.

"Our Green Garden" touched American readers because it depends on an underlying worldview that is at the heart of the constitution of the Beloved Community: the interconnectedness of all things through love. Love, more than blood, makes family, and the speaker in "Our Green Garden" is in a heartfelt colloquy with his "brother," someone who has taken up arms against him, despite the fact that they have the same mother (Vietnam). The same distortions that sundered one Vietnamese from another had separated Americans from the Vietnamese, though all were members of the Beloved Community. King and Nhat Hanh meeting in Chicago was the coming together, the reconciliation of brothers. It is worth reproducing "Our Green Garden" here—it is a beautiful poem that had a far-reaching and powerful effect on the American public and backgrounds the familial relationship between all who are loyal to the Beloved Community.

Our Green Garden

Fires spring up at all ten points of the universe.
A furious, acrid wind sweeps them toward us from all sides.
Aloof and beautiful, the mountains and rivers abide.

All around, the horizon burns with the color of death.
As for me, yes, I am still alive,
but my body and soul writhe as if they too had been set on fire.
My parched eyes can shed no more tears.

Where are you going this evening, dear brother, in what direction?
The rattle of gunfire is close at hand.
In her breast, the heart of our mother shrivels and
fades like a dying flower.
She bows her head,
her smooth black hair now threaded with white.
How many nights has she crouched, wide awake,
alone with her lantern, praying for the storm to end?

Dearest brother, I know it is you who will shoot me tonight,
piercing our mother's heart with a wound that can never heal.
O terrible winds that blow from the ends of the Earth,
hurling down our houses and blasting our fertile fields!

I say farewell to the blazing, blackening place where I was born.
Here is my breast! Aim your gun at it, brother, shoot!
I offer my body, the body our mother bore and nurtured.
Destroy it if you wish.
Destroy it in the name of your dream—
that dream in whose name you kill.

Can you hear me invoke the darkness,
"When will the suffering end?
O darkness, in whose name do you destroy?"

Come back, dear brother, and kneel at our mother's knee.
Don't sacrifice our green garden
to the ragged flames that have been carried into the front yard
by wild winds from far away.

Here is my breast. Aim your gun at it, brother, shoot!
Destroy me if you wish
and build from my carrion
whatever it is you are dreaming of.

Who will be left to celebrate a victory made of blood and fire?

It is hard to know what American readers made of the Buddhist cosmological reference, "the ten points of the universe," but in all likelihood they felt keenly the sorrow of one people being torn apart, as if brothers had forgotten their common origin and become enemies. The grandparents of many Americans in the 1950s and '60s may have been children in the American Civil War. The grandparents of many Black Americans during the civil rights movement of the 1950s and '60s may have been enslaved children or themselves the children of slaves—people betrayed for generations by their own country. The homegrown American experience of the unity of a people, its interrelatedness, being ripped apart may have surfaced by reading "Our Green Garden."

On balance, then, there are forces we can trace moving Nhat Hanh and King toward one another, as well as countervailing forces that would make their friendship unlikely. That their meetings, exchanges, and friendship came forth despite these walls is a testimony to their will, courage, and foresight.

Concepts of Martyrdom in the Cause of Love

As we saw in the opening of this book, the first communication between Nhat Hanh and King was occasioned by a series of events in Vietnam in the early 1960s that shocked the world, galvanized Buddhists in Vietnam, and still has the power to unsettle people today: the self-immolations of Buddhists beginning in 1963. In reference to the photograph of Thich Quang Duc on fire, John F. Kennedy said: "No news picture in history has generated so much emotion around the world as that one."[51] The pictures of the self-immolations and the accompanying news stories could not capture the substance behind these iconic actions. Though the self-immolations were widely viewed as suicides in the Western press, the truth was quite different—they were witnessing for religious freedom and peace.[52]

These self-immolations began with the death of Thich Quang Duc on June 11, 1963.[53] Three more Buddhists burned themselves to death that summer.[54] Sister Chan Khong, who witnessed Thich Quang Duc's death, wrote of the path of growing commitment that led Nhat Chi Mai, a "sister in the Dharma" to Chan Khong, to self-immolate on May 16, 1967.[55] In her book *Learning True Love,* Sister Chan Khong recognizes that self-immolation is difficult for Westerners to understand, especially as they learned about them in newspaper articles describing them as suicides. However, the category of suicide is profoundly misleading here, because the self-immolations of Buddhists were not acts of despair; on the contrary, they were sacrificial acts of total love.[56]

The nature of this total love could manifest in scandalously material ways, a story that strains the credulity of some who have heard it, but one which points to the enormous energy contained in these acts of self-sacrifice. Such acts have the power to ring and reverberate in the minds not only of those who witness them in person, but for people who hear about them later. Consider the following story Sister Chan Khong shared with me in an interview in 2019. She makes a startling claim about Thich Quang Duc's funeral, held on June 20, 1963, which was attended by thousands of Vietnamese. Quang Duc's badly burned body was cremated, but "after six hours of cremation, all of Thich Quang Duc's body had become ash, except his heart, which was still reddish-brown and intact. After a second cremation, at 1,000° C, his heart remained exactly the same shape, although an even darker color."[57]

I asked Sister Chan Khong what she thought the survival of Thich Quang Duc's heart through two cremations meant, and she answered me, "His heart was completely love, and so, imperishable."[58]

This imperishable love expressed itself with terrifying power in the self-immolations of the 1960s, acts that were not an abandonment of love but its continuation in radical form. Both in *Learning True Love* and in her interviews with me in Hue, Sister Chan Khong said that the acts of self-immolation in Vietnam in the early 1960s unleashed hundreds of acts of love and compassion.[59] I was reminded of A. J. Muste's striking proposition, that "whenever love that will suffer unto death . . . is manifested unconquerable power is released into the stream of history."[60] This tide of love's power is not at all the last act of a person who has given up all hope but comes from a fullness, an overflowing of love.

Burning in Buddhist Monastic Ordinations in Vietnam

In his letter about the self-immolations to King, Nhat Hanh mentions that, during their ordinations, Buddhist novices sometimes undergo a ritual in which they burn small spots on their skin. This ritual is not only, as Nhat Hanh says, expressive of seriousness of purpose but is also—though it may perhaps strangely to our ears—a kind of healing.

Two strands of Chinese history interweave to create the healing quality of burning at ordination: *moxa* burning and a Buddhist figure called the Medicine King. Moxa is an herbal preparation that had been used in China even before Buddhism arrived in the country. It is burned in spots on the skin to influence the flow of energy through the body, which promotes healing. The Medicine King was a bodhisattva who, to express his gratitude to the Buddha, anointed himself with perfumes for many years, and when saturated with the scents—that is, when he had himself become an incense offering—he set himself on fire.[61] James Benn speculates that the moxibustion references in Chinese Buddhist sutras that validate burning at ordination, combined with the foundational references to the self-immolation of a bodhisattva named Medicine King, point to self-immolation as an act of healing.[62]

But healing from what? The healing being worked in the Buddhist ordinations is a spiritual healing—healing from the delusions of the world. One of these delusions is that of separateness, the denial of fundamental interconnectedness.

From early in his career, Thich Nhat Hanh viewed his purpose as an ordained Buddhist monk to be the reviving of Buddhism in Vietnam—what he called "Engaged Buddhism." First, Nhat Hanh applied a nondual view to peace in Vietnam; peace was not to be achieved by the dominance of either the South or the North, but by seeing the country as a whole. Healing, then, would be the realization of a nondual view of the country.

At a practical level, Thich Nhat Hanh thought that Vietnam could be healed by Buddhist monastics becoming active agents of social change among the Vietnamese people and that the monks and nuns could connect directly with the suffering of the Vietnamese people.[63] He encouraged young Buddhists to move beyond the giving of alms or charity and to actively embrace the sort of social work that would equip the Vietnamese people to move out of poverty.[64] Because this was such a radical vision of Buddhism—one that aimed at social transformation rather than mere preservation—it was bound to elicit resistance. Indeed, in his published journals, *Fragrant Palm Leaves*, Nhat Hanh measures the level of innovation that Engaged Buddhism represented by the degree of opposition his efforts received from the Buddhist authorities.[65]

In my interviews with Sister Chan Khong, she emphasized that the acts that flowed from the self-immolations were acts of "formless love." When I asked her what she meant by this formlessness, she said that the loving acts were formless in that they were not imitative, but rather creative responses. The self-immolations did not inspire imitation—that is, thousands of other self-immolations—but rather they inspired thousands of acts of compassion for the healing of the people and the country. The goal of the self-immolations was to release creative energies that would move Vietnam toward a better future.

King's Reception of Nhat Hanh's Letter on Self-Immolation

How did King understand Nhat Hanh's letter on self-immolation? He would have had to overcome Western religious and cultural norms that condemned self-destruction as suicide, and in addition to that, he would have had to move beyond the views of his mentor in nonviolence, A. J. Muste, who, as we have seen, had a great influence on King's understanding and practice of nonviolence. Muste said that nonviolent activists should be willing to face violence and suffering, even death, but they must not deliberately seek out suffering: "Martyrdom for the sake of martyrdom is suicide by exhibitionism, not redemptive crucifixion."[66] The martyrdom of the prophets—in the Hebrew scriptures and in the New Testament—provided a frame within which King could understand Nhat Hanh's explanation of self-immolation as total commitment to the cause of love and as healing.

The most important reference to martyrdom in King's life would have been scriptural. The Beatitudes are found, in two different forms, in the Gospels of Matthew and Luke.[67] Both versions are famous within the Christian tradition, and both end with a pronouncement of blessing on those who are persecuted "for righteousness sake, . . . for in the same way they persecuted the prophets who were before you."[68] Jesus repeats the trope of the persecution of the prophets throughout the Gospels, often sharpening it to include persecution unto death:

Jerusalem, Jerusalem, the city that kills the prophets and stones those who are sent to it! How often have I desired to gather your children together as a hen gathers her brood under her wings, and you were not willing! See, your house is left to you, desolate. For I tell you, you will not see me again until you say, "Blessed is the one who comes in the name of the Lord."[69]

In the Gospels and in the New Testament as a whole, these invocations of persecution not only look backward to the prophets but also forward to the crucifixion, thus giving all New Testament persecution language a Christological shape that would have profoundly influenced King, a child of preachers and a preacher himself.

In addition to King's own understanding of key passages about prophets and martyrdom that he would have gathered through Christian worship and study, it is likely that he was also exposed to the work of Abraham Joshua Heschel on the role and function of prophets in ancient Israel.[70] In Heschel's influential 1962 book, *The Prophets*, Heschel presented a powerful vision of the Hebrew prophets: neither primarily seers nor soothsayers, the Hebrew prophets were those who proclaimed and manifested God's own righteousness and justice toward the poor and oppressed.[71]

Righteousness, according to Heschel's reading of the core qualities of the Hebrew prophets, is associated with a "burning compassion for the oppressed," while *justice* is the application of righteousness in the life of Israel. While the center of righteousness may be said to be compassion, justice is exacting.[72] But the prophets are not judges, in Heschel's view. Rather, they are upholding a way of life for the whole community, a way of life characterized by righteousness and justice, as contrasted to the delivering of particular remedies to discrete transgressions.[73]

Heschel eloquently sums up the meaning of prophecy in ancient Israel:

> *Prophecy is the voice that God has lent to the silent agony, a voice to the plundered poor, to the profane riches of the world. It is a form of living, a crossing point of God and man. God is raging in the prophet's words.*[74]

As there is a world patterned by God's precepts and the covenants God has established to memorialize them, so too there is a world opposed to God. There are the poor, and they suffer agony; there is a profane world of enormous wealth; and the juxtaposition of these two worlds exposes breaches of justice that cause God to rage. Prophetic mission is the divine response to the divided and divisive world, but the courageous exercise of the prophetic mission will call down the wrath of the world—the result being martyrdom.

Given Heschel's prominence as a religious scholar in mid-twentieth century America and the publication date of *The Prophets*, we might expect that King would share the view of the prophetic call and its consequences sketched previously. And there are further reasons that could confirm this possibility: Heschel and King were both speakers at a United Synagogue of America convention in 1963; at this convention King supported Heschel in advocating for just and fair treatment for Jews in the Soviet Union; Heschel was in the front lines of the Selma March in 1965; and, King and Heschel were both signers of a call for the end of the Vietnam War in 1967.[75] King and Heschel were close allies in acute American struggles for justice, and that King would know and affirm Heschel's view of prophecy, prophets, and martyrdom is to be expected.

Heschel's *The Prophets*, however, would only have solidified and coalesced King's understanding of the role of prophets and of martyrdom, if it played any role at all. King was deeply imbued in a Christian theology that placed the witness of the prophets of the Hebrew scriptures calling for, and demanding justice. In both his "Letter from a Birmingham Jail" and in his "I Have a Dream" speech given at the March on Washington in 1963, King quotes the prophet Amos 5:24, "Let justice roll down like waters and righteousness like a mighty stream."

But for the deepest confirmation of King's view of the prophet and of martyrdom, we must turn to his last speech, delivered in Memphis on the evening of April 3, 1968, the speech called "I Have Been to the Mountaintop." King had come to Memphis for a march to be held on April 4 in support of striking sanitation workers. He frames his speech with an allusion to Moses, the paradigmatic Hebrew prophet. In the Book of Deuteronomy, God takes the aged Moses up Mount Nebo, across the Jordan River from the land to which God had been leading the Hebrew people for forty years. God says to Moses, "I have let you see it with your eyes, but you will not cross into it."[76] Between these two reference points—outraged Amos calling his people back to the ways of God and the impending death of Moses as narrated in Deuteronomy—we see King's self-understanding as being someone who stands in the line of the prophets, both carrying their typical message and suffering their fate of martyrdom.

While this final sermon is full of metaphors and historical and cultural references, the prevailing metaphoric theme is the Exodus. King opens the theme by saying,

> *I would take my mental flight by Egypt and I would watch God's children in their magnificent trek from the dark dungeons of Egypt through, or rather across the Red Sea, through the wilderness on toward the promised land.*[77]

At the end of the sermon, King returns, emotionally, to the metaphorical theme. He tells the audience that on the tarmac before his flight for Memphis, there had been a delay before takeoff, and the captain had informed the passengers that it was due to the necessity of checking everyone's bags for security, because "we have Dr. Martin Luther King on the plane." And then King goes on to say that when he got to Memphis, he began hearing rumors of threats against his life. And he concludes,

Well, I don't know what will happen now. We've got some difficult days ahead. But it really doesn't matter with me now, because I've been to the mountaintop. And I don't mind. . . . I just want to do God's will. And He's allowed me to go up to the mountain. And I've looked over. And I've seen the Promised Land. I may not get there with you. But I want you to know tonight, that we, as a people, will get to the Promised Land![78]

King is comparing himself to Moses, who led God's people out of Egypt, spent forty years in the wilderness, and who, on "verge of the Jordan," was allowed only to look upon the land his followers would inhabit. King is accepting the role of the prophet and fate of the prophet—martyrdom.[79]

Thich Nhat Hanh reached out to King from his own context, explaining that there was a background for self-immolation of Thich Quang Duc and others in the ordination rites of Buddhist monks in India, China, and Vietnam. King received the letter from Nhat Hanh in another religious and cultural context, that of the Hebrew prophets and Jesus of Nazareth, who bequeathed the prophet's role to his followers.[80]

The equating of those Buddhists who self-immolated in Vietnam in the 1960s with the martyrs of the civil rights movement in the United States—even though affirmed by King—remains a matter of some controversy. The prohibition in Western culture against suicide is deeply entrenched and hard to overcome. While Nhat Hanh made a powerful argument to reframe the self-immolations, it was King's own life position after years in the thick of the civil rights movement that enabled him to understand and accept the argument. King's position was akin to that of Jesus in relation to his disciples. Jesus's choices took him closer and closer to peril, to exposure to the Roman empire's censure, and to his own martyrdom. He could see the consequences of his choices, but even his most intimate followers are presented in the Gospels as not understanding the danger. A clear example of this is found in the Gospel of Mark (8:31–38):

> *Then he began to teach them that the Son of Man must undergo great suffering, and be rejected by the elders, the chief priests, and the scribes, and be killed, and after three days rise again. He said all this quite openly. And Peter took him aside and began to rebuke him. But turning and looking at his disciples, he rebuked Peter and said, "Get behind me, Satan! For you are setting your mind not on divine things but on human things."*
>
> *He called the crowd with his disciples, and said to them, "If any want to become my followers, let them deny themselves and take up their cross and follow me. For those who want to save their life will lose it, and those who lose their life for my sake, and for the sake of the gospel, will save it. For what will it profit them to gain the whole world and forfeit their life? Indeed, what can they give in return for their life? Those who are ashamed of me and of my words in this adulterous and sinful generation, of them the Son of Man will also be ashamed when he comes in the glory of his Father with the holy angels."*

Despite the disciples' closeness to Jesus and the danger they themselves were in by being associated with him, there remained a yawning gulf between their existential awareness of what it meant to be a follower of Jesus and Jesus's own awareness of his eventual martyrdom. King seemed keenly aware that his own martyrdom was nearing, and so he was able to grasp the equation of the self-immolations in Vietnam as the same kind of acts of total commitment to a cause (and acts of healing) as he hoped his own life choices were.

It was also likely that King's increasing experience of being a world citizen, one who glimpsed and began to give his heart to the Beloved Community, that allowed King to make this leap of identification between the self-immolations in Vietnam and Christian martyrdom. Particularly, King's 1959 trip to India helped him to gain a sense of solidarity with oppressed people of color everywhere—just as similar trips to India had done for Thurman and other Black leaders. Nhat Hanh appeals to this commonality in his letter:

> Now in the confrontation of the big powers occurring in our country, hundreds and perhaps thousands of Vietnamese peasants and children lose their lives every day, and our land is unmercifully and tragically torn by a war which is already twenty years old. I am sure that since you have been engaged in one of the hardest struggles for equality and human rights, you are among those who understand fully, and who share with all their hearts, the indescribable suffering of the Vietnamese people.[81]

Thich Nhat Hanh is making an appeal based on a special case of the interrelatedness of all life, that is, the interrelatedness of all oppressed people. In the way of a true peacemaker, however, Nhat Hanh does not make an enemy of the oppressors in the Vietnam War; the true enemies are not people, but ignorance, fear, and hatred. Even the oppressor could be healed and take a place back in the Beloved Community.

King was not led to an opposition to the Vietnam War by Nhat Hanh alone; he had made his own withering analysis of the hypocrisy of a war that disproportionately depended on Black soldiers, who were good enough to be wounded and die for their country, but who returned, if they returned at all, to systemic and institutionalized racism.[82] What Nhat Hanh brought to King was the reality of solidarity in struggle and suffering between African Americans and the Vietnamese.

Whether or not the inner reasons that brought Nhat Hanh and King together over the Vietnam War have been parsed correctly, still it is true that upon their first meeting, on May 31, 1966, they issued a joint statement that equated those who died in the nonviolent cause of justice and peace in Vietnam to the martyrs in the American struggle for African American civil rights.[83]

Friendship and Common Cause

A J. Muste, working on behalf of the Fellowship of Rec-
. onciliation, arranged a meeting between Nhat Hanh and
King in Chicago on May 31, 1966. They conferred privately for
some time, discussing the latest crises in Vietnam, and then held
a joint press conference at the Sheraton-Chicago Hotel.[84] The
paradoxical nature of this meeting is that there are no detailed
notes on the private conversation and no transcript or recording
of the press conference is known at this time. In an interview
with Oprah Winfrey, Thich Nhat Hanh recalled, "We had a discussion about peace, freedom, and community. And we agreed
that without a community, we cannot go very far."[85]

The main artifacts of the 1966 meeting are photographs of
Nhat Hanh and King at the press conference. The power of these
photographs is felt immediately: the men have an intensity of
expression, and their youthful energy radiates from them. If the
photographs can be considered to have iconic quality, it would
be of friendship and solidarity. They are not two men working
on isolated issues; the message is their commitment and their
common cause.

May 31, 1966: Press photo of Ray Gould, Martin Luther King Jr., and Thich Nhat Hanh in Chicago.

At some point that day, likely during the press conference, they released a joint statement. The statement read:

We believe that the Buddhists who have sacrificed themselves, like the martyrs of the civil rights movement, do not aim at the injury of the oppressors but only at changing their policies. The enemies of those struggling for freedom and democracy are not man. They are discrimination, dictatorship, greed, hatred and violence, which lie within the heart of man. These are the real enemies of man—not man himself.

We also believe that the struggles for equality and freedom in Birmingham, Selma and Chicago, as in Hue, Danang and Saigon, are aimed not at the domination of one people by another. They are aimed at self-determination, peaceful social change, and a better life for all human beings. And we believe that only in a world of peace can the work of construction, of building good societies everywhere, go forward.

We join in the plea, written June 1, 1965, by Thich Nhat Hanh in a letter to Martin Luther King, Jr., 'Do not kill man, even in man's name. Please kill the real enemies of man which are present everywhere, in our very hearts and minds.'"

International Committee of Conscien-
on Vietnam
Box 271, Nyack, New York

Contact:
    Alfred Hassler
    Box 271
    Nyack, New York
    Phone: NYC CO-7-3262

r

    Paul Lauter
    431 South Dearborn
    Chicago, Illinois 60605
    Phone: HA 7-2533
         549-0774
         NO 7-6185

or Release: IMMEDIATE

    Dr. Martin Luther King, Jr., Nobel Peace Prize winner, conferred today in Chicago wit: leading South Vietnamese Buddhist monk. The monk, Thich Nhat Hanh, is risking his life : oming to the United States to ask for peace in Vietnam.

    Dr. King and Thich Nhat Hanh issued the following statement at the conclusion of their eeting:

    "We believe that the Buddhists who have sacrificed themselves, like the martyrs of the civil rights movement, do not aim at the injury of the oppressors but only at changing their policies. The enemies of those struggling for freedom and democracy are not man. They are discrimination, dictatorship, greed, hatred and violence, which lie within the heart of man. These are the real enemies of man -- not man himself.

    "We also believe that the struggles for equality and freedom in Birmingham, Selma and Chicago, as in Hue, Danang and Saigon, are aimed not at the domination of one people by another. The are aimed at self-determination, peaceful social change, and a better life for all human beings. And we believe that only in a world of peace can the work of construction, of building good societies everywhere, go forward.

    "We join in the plea written June 1, 1965, by Thich Nhat Hanh in a letter to Martin Luther King, Jr., 'Do not kill man, even in man's name. Please kill

Typewritten notice following the press conference, containing the first part of their joint statement.

This brief statement of mutuality and solidarity bursts with meaning; in it, deaths that had been conceived of as suicides are redefined as martyrs' deaths. Further, common cause is made between those in the Vietnamese peace movement and Black civil rights activists. For some, the fact that Nhat Hanh was not a partisan for either North or South Vietnam must surely have been lost in the seeming enormity of King making a joint statement with a representative of a country at war with the United States. Living in the Beloved Community meant, for King, living in what he called "the World House," or as Nhat Hanh would express it, "becoming a citizen of the world." King believed that living in the World House didn't mean abandoning his national and local causes, but whatever he personally believed, the wider public wondered if King was trading civil rights for Blacks for peace for Vietnam, and other international causes, such as international justice.

To make this statement together, on their first meeting, was an extraordinary step in their relationship. At the May 31, 1966, meeting, with its private conversation followed by the press conference, we may say that Nhat Hanh and King began a friendship that is at the heart of the Beloved Community to which both men dedicated their lives.*

---

* During my last set of interviews with senior members of Nhat Hanh's community in Hue, Vietnam, in 2019, I was astounded to hear that among papers of Nhat Hanh's that may never be made public, there is a letter that was given by King to Nhat Hanh during that meeting in Chicago. The letter was in a sealed envelope, and King told Nhat Hanh not to open it until after they had left the meeting. Both men were on flights to Washington, DC, after the press conference, for different reasons—Nhat Hanh was beginning a speaking tour to inform the US public about the war in Vietnam, and King was to attend a White House conference. According to the Buddhist nun who told me about it, the brief letter from King was an assurance that theirs was a friendship based on love. I am choosing not to name the sister who was the source for this narrative, as, when I asked if I might see the letter, she said that Nhat Hanh may never permit, even after his death, for a whole body of papers related to his life to be made public, including this letter. I am trying to honor what was presented to me as deeply personal communication, while still referencing the appearance of friendship and love in the letter.

Soon after this press conference, which was part of a larger campaign to call for an end to hostilities in Vietnam, the governments of North and South Vietnam denied Nhat Hanh the right to return home, and he began a long exile of thirty-nine years.

The Nobel Peace Prize Nomination, January 25, 1967

It is well known that Martin Luther King Jr. nominated Thich Nhat Hanh for the 1967 Nobel Peace Prize, a fact frequently mentioned whenever their relationship is the subject of news articles.[86] There are several parts of the letter that are widely quoted. One of them is: "I know Thich Nhat Hanh, and am privileged to call him my friend."

He goes on to write:

> *Thich Nhat Hanh today is virtually homeless and stateless. If he were to return to Vietnam, which he passionately wishes to do, his life would be in great peril. He is the victim of a particularly brutal exile because he proposes to carry his advocacy of peace to his own people. What a tragic commentary this is on the existing situation in Vietnam and those who perpetuate it.*
>
> *The history of Vietnam is filled with chapters of exploitation by outside powers and corrupted men of wealth, until even now the Vietnamese are harshly ruled, ill-fed, poorly housed, and burdened by all the hardships and terrors of modern warfare.*
>
> *Thich Nhat Hanh offers a way out of this nightmare, a solution acceptable to rational leaders. He has traveled the world, counseling statesmen, religious leaders, scholars and writers, and enlisting their support. His ideas for peace, if applied, would build a monument to ecumenism, to world brotherhood, to humanity.*

Like Nhat Hanh's letter to King regarding the self-immolation of the Buddhist monastics in Vietnam, King's nomination of Nhat Hanh was in the form of a public letter, which was highly unusual as a nomination. Of the more than one hundred articles online that I examined that mentioned the peace prize nomination, none of them speculates as to why King made his nomination public. Another highly unusual aspect of the 1967 Nobel Peace Prize is that no prize was actually awarded that year.

The rules established for nominating people for the prize specify not only who may submit nominations (former laureates, such as King, are among those who may do so), but also the terms of the nominations, importantly that the Nobel Foundation officially keeps the names of both the nominators and the nominees secret for a period of fifty years from the year of the prize in question. It is hard to believe that King did not know that the Nobel Foundation forbade public nominations. Assuming that King was well aware of the rules, what may have been the reason for his choice to make his nomination public?

In his 1963 "Letter from a Birmingham Jail," King answers a question he puts on the lips of the addressees of the letter, "Wouldn't negotiation be better than direct action?" Here is how King answers this rhetorical question:

> You may well ask, "Why direct action, why sit-ins, marches, and so forth? Isn't negotiation a better path?" You are exactly right in your call for negotiation. Indeed, this is the purpose of direct action. Nonviolent direct action seeks to create such a crisis and establish such creative tension that a community that has consistently refused to negotiate is forced to confront the issue. It seeks so to dramatize the issue that it can no longer be ignored.

King turns the subject of negotiation around and points out that the white leadership of Birmingham has been refusing to negotiate with Blacks: "We . . . concur with you in your call for negotiation. Too long has our beloved Southland been bogged down in the tragic attempt to live in monologue rather than dialogue."[87]

The nonviolent action theory that King inherited from Gandhi, Muste, and others, a theory refined and deployed with

Glenn Smiley and Bayard Rustin, included this notion of "creat(ing) such a crisis and establish(ing) such creative tension." The letter itself is an example of "constructive nonviolent tension" in that, though its primary addressees were prominent White clergy in Birmingham, it was a public letter. Publishing it as an open letter, we must imagine, placed enormous pressure on these clergy; their dinner conversations were surely filled with tension! If King had written them privately and confidentially, these Birmingham clergy might have chosen to ignore King.

Once we place King's public nomination of Nhat Hanh in the company of the "Letter from a Birmingham Jail," and other nonviolent actions that he led in the civil rights movement, we can surmise that King was seeking more than to honor Nhat Hanh and their shared goal of peace between the United States and Vietnam. Additionally, King was raising the tension in the international community, calling for courage to risk the displeasure of both the Communist allies of the Viet Cong and the Western allies of the United States and to stand for peace.

Viewed in this way, King's public nomination of Nhat Hanh for the 1967 Nobel Peace Prize is far weightier than the suggestion of an honor to a person he may have admired from afar; King is acting in the kind of loving solidarity with Nhat Hanh as he acted with his friends in the civil rights movement.*

Just as articles about the nomination do not question why King made his nomination public, there is also a lack of speculation as to why the prize committee did not make an award in 1967. To answer this next question, we turn again to the "Letter from a Birmingham Jail."

---

* Note how King opens his last speech, the great "I Have Been to the Mountaintop" speech, *It's always good to have your closest friend and associate say something good about you. And Ralph Abernathy is the best friend I have in the world.* King is not making the polite public thanks we may customarily hear after even a fulsome introduction.

If the clergymen who were the addressees of King's letter ever responded, publicly or privately, their responses have been buried in the records of history. If this is the case and the clergy did not respond, it seems reasonable that civil society would take their silence as an admission of the truth contained in King's letter. The brilliance of King's rhetorical device, of this instance of raising the tension, lies in a consideration of who King intended his real audience to be. The final, most consequential audience for the Letter is the reading public. You can imagine this public waiting, with differing expectations, for the responses of the named addressees, the clergy leaders in Birmingham. When no answer comes, the public is left to sort out what this means, whose case and cause stands up in the end.

After King had made a public nomination of Nhat Hanh, a nomination from surely one of the most prominent peace and justice advocates of the time, himself the 1964 laureate, could the prize committee have selected anyone else? Yes, King "broke the rules," but wouldn't such a transgression have stood public scrutiny as justification for awarding the prize to someone else? What I think we may conclude is that the 1967 Peace Prize nomination is an unheralded success for King in nonviolent action on the international stage. The failure of the prize committee to make an award in 1967 showed the world that they were either too beholden or too afraid to make Nhat Hanh the laureate.* Why would we believe that King's letter nominating Nhat Hanh for the Nobel Peace Prize was anything other than well-thought out?

---

* I have reviewed the history of the Nobel Peace Prizes, which date back to 1901. There are gaps in the awarding of the prizes, notably during World Wars I and II. Others gaps include 1923, 1924, 1928, 1932, 1948 (a gap that the committee attributed to their being "no suitable living candidate," a nod to the recently assassinated Gandhi), 1955, 1956, 1966, and 1972. This list is small in a 118-year history, making each absence notable. This very rarity when combined with the arguments I have made in the main text of the dissertation points to the possibility of King's action being a deliberate instance of nonviolent action.

"Beyond Vietnam," April 4, 1967

Thich Nhat Hanh has said that King "spoke out for the first time" against the Vietnam War at their joint press conference in Chicago in 1966.[88] The *King Encyclopedia*, however, chronicles King's open questioning of and opposition to the war dating back to 1965. I think the case can be made that King's arguments against the war at least changed character after his friendship with Nhat Hanh began.

First, King expanded his arguments against the war. In 1965 King called for a halt in the bombings of North Vietnam, arguing that the United States must take steps to build mutual trust between the two countries; in the same year, King voiced his disapproval based on his stance as a Christian minister—"As a minister of the gospel I consider war an evil. I must cry out when I see war escalated at any point." He also critiqued the war based on the racism faced by African American soldiers and the hypocrisy of condemnations of African American violence in urban riots while the country overall approved of a massively violent war against the Vietnamese people.

After the 1966 meeting and press conference with Thich Nhat Hanh, King's arguments more and more sought to highlight and bring to the consciousness of the people of the United States the reality of the war for the Vietnamese people, an argument put forward first to him in the open letter from Nhat Hanh on the self-immolations. At root, this new content and emphasis by King is based on interdependence: the Vietnamese are our brothers and sisters. King's willingness to promote two new ideas—first, that the Vietnamese people are part of our life, and we are part of their life; and second, that if we have an enemy, it is not the Vietnamese people—tells us that King's friendship with Nhat Hanh was both personal and rooted within the Beloved Community.

And though King had been speaking out in opposition to the Vietnam War before the 1966 press conference and before the sermon in Riverside Church in New York City, that speech, "Beyond Vietnam," was something new. The extensive nature of the arguments in "Beyond Vietnam," their careful reasoning, and their unrelenting tone drew King widespread criticism, including from within the civil rights movement itself.[89] With "Beyond Vietnam," King shows his willingness to be a martyr in loyalty to another manifestation, beyond the local, of the Beloved Community.

King took aim at what he saw as an underlying moral rot that guides American foreign policy: ". . . the need to maintain social stability for our investments . . . [the refusal] to give up the privileges and the pleasures that come from the immense profits of overseas investments." "Beyond Vietnam" did not represent an abandonment of King's commitment to combating racism—on the contrary, in this sermon he takes his analysis of racism to a deeper level: "When machines and computers, profit motives and property rights, are considered more important than people, the giant triplets of racism, extreme materialism, and militarism are incapable of being conquered."

Finally, "Beyond Vietnam" seems to contain a reference to Nhat Hanh:

> *This is the message of the great Buddhist leaders of Vietnam. Recently one of them wrote these words, and I quote: "Each day the war goes on, the hatred increased in the hearts of the Vietnamese and in the hearts of those of humanitarian instinct. The Americans are forcing even their friends into becoming their enemies. It is curious that the Americans, who calculate so carefully on the possibilities of military victory, do not realize that in the process they are incurring deep psychological and political defeat. The image of America will never again be the image of revolution, freedom, and democracy, but the image of violence and militarism."[90]*

I do not claim that Thich Nhat Hanh brought the Vietnam War to King's attention; King had made his own penetrating analysis of the injustice of the war in terms of racial prejudice—the United States was glad to accept the lives of young Black soldiers in the active war effort, but the country neglected those who survived, who returned home to a country marked by segregation and racial violence against Black people.[91] What I have attempted to show, rather, is that Nhat Hanh both sharpened and broadened King's opposition to the war. Due in large measure to Nhat Hanh's influence, King began to see the injustice of the war as also stemming from injustice to the people of Vietnam, not only to Blacks in the United States.

World Council of Churches Pacem in Terris Conference, May 1967

Pacem in Terris (Peace on Earth) was the last papal encyclical of Pope John XXIII. It was issued on April 11, 1963, two months before the pope's death. *Pacem in Terris* marked a new phase for papal encyclicals; Pope John XXIII broke with tradition in not relying solely on Catholic scholastic theological bases; instead, he turned to events of the day to which he sought to respond. Rather than rely heavily on natural law, he shifted to situational ethics. His audience, too, was new; rather than being addressed specifically to the Catholic faithful, *Pacem in Terris* was addressed to "people of good will." All of the above—the method, the theme, and the audience—garnered immense public attention. One year later, the United Nations held a conference on human rights inspired by the encyclical, and of the same name. Other Pacem in Terris conferences, hosted by other organizations, followed.

In May 1967 the World Council of Churches held a Pacem in Terris conference in Geneva, Switzerland, and Nhat Hanh and King both attended. The *New York Times* reported that King delivered a "bitter denunciation" of the Vietnam War there. The conference was also the last time that King and Nhat Hanh would meet. Their meeting may be seen as a metaphysical exchange between friends, marked by human warmth and humor. Here is how Nhat Hanh describes their meeting:

> *Dr. King was staying on the eleventh floor; I was on the fourth floor. He invited me up for breakfast. On my way, I was detained by the press, so I arrived late. He had kept the breakfast warm for me and had waited for me. I greeted him, "Dr. King, Dr. King!"*
>
> *"Dr. Hanh, Dr. Hanh!" he replied.*
>
> *We were able to continue our discussion on peace, freedom, and community, and what kind of steps America could take to end the war. And we agreed that without a community, we cannot go very far. Without a happy, harmonious community, we will not be able to realize our dream.*
>
> *I said to him, "Martin, do you know something? In Vietnam they call you a bodhisattva, an enlightened being trying to awaken other living beings and help them move toward more compassion and understanding." I'm glad I had the chance to tell him that, because just a few months later he was assassinated in Memphis.*[92]

According to Sister Chan Khong, it was at the Pacem in Terris meeting that King shared his understanding of the Beloved Community with Thich Nhat Hanh.[93] The importance of community was a mutual value for the two men; in fact, Sister Chan Khong holds that since before his ordination at the age of sixteen, Nhat Hanh has worked for "true sisterhood and brotherhood" in Vietnam.

In return, Thich Nhat Hanh tells King that he is viewed as a "bodhisattva" in Vietnam, an enlightened being with the quality of awakening compassion in others. King is not the only person Nhat Hanh calls a bodhisattva. In other places, he calls the Earth, the Sun, the mother of the Buddha, and Sister Chan Khong "bodhisattvas." The designation by Nhat Hanh of non-traditional bodhisattvas is far more than a personal, affectionate bestowing of an honorific. Nhat Hanh is advancing his ideas of the restoration and reformation of Buddhism by his expansion of the beings who may be venerated as bodhisattvas. In Thich Nhat Hanh's communities, well-known bodhisattvas, venerated throughout the Mahayana, are honored too, resettling the landscape of the holy. For instance, by invoking the mother of the Buddha and Sister Chan Khong, Thich Nhat Hanh honors human women.

A central goal of his reform of Buddhism in Vietnam has been gender equality in monastic Buddhism, and the honoring of a human woman as a bodhisattva furthers that goal. King, as a Christian American, might be another challenging entry into the lists of the holy for Vietnamese Buddhists, when placed next to the legendary bodhisattvas Manjushri and Avalokiteshvara.* Both King and Sister Chan Khong are also people of the contemporary world, bringing the idea of the holy close. The Earth and the Sun as bodhisattvas are in keeping with Nhat Hanh's contributions to the Beloved Community; with Nhat Hanh, the concept is completely inclusive—all human life, all life we recognize as sentient, all beings of the cosmos.

As to what King made of Nhat Hanh's telling King that he is a bodhisattva during their Geneva meeting, we can hope that this message of respect and affirmation was a comfort to King as he faced the challenges of what would be the last months of his life.

---

* Both Manjushri and Avalokiteshvara are deities, the former being the embodiment of wisdom. Avalokiteshvara, in Sanskrit is a lord who looks down on and is attentive to the cries of the suffering world; in other words, Avalokiteshvara is divine compassion. When Buddhism was carried into China, Avalokiteshvara's name became Guanyin, or later, Kuanyin, the goddess of compassion. Both Manjushri and Avalokiteshvara, then, are of an entirely different order of being—divinities—from several of the people Nhat Hanh has called bodhisattvas, like Sister Chan Khong and Martin Luther King Jr.

I Have Always Felt His Support

The day after King's "I Have Been to the Mountaintop" sermon, he was assassinated on the balcony of the Lorraine Motel in Memphis. With him were several close friends and coworkers in the civil rights movement, Andrew Young, Ralph Abernathy, and Jesse Jackson. The morning after hearing the news, Thich Nhat Hanh wrote a heartbroken letter to their mutual friend Raphael Gould, one of the directors of the Fellowship of Reconciliation: "I did not sleep last night. . . . They killed Martin Luther King. They killed us. I am afraid the root of violence is so deep in the heart and mind and manner of this society. They killed him. They killed my hope. I do not know what to say. . . . He made so great an impression in me. This morning I have the impression that I cannot bear the loss."

Years later, Thich Nhat Hanh recalled: "I was in New York when I heard the news of his assassination; I was devastated. I could not eat; I could not sleep. I made a deep vow to continue building what he called 'the beloved community,' not only for myself but for him also. I have done what I promised to Martin Luther King Jr. And I think that I have always felt his support."[94]

4/5/1918
Dear Ray,

I did not sleep last night; I tried to contact you through Lee at the FOR but the line was not available.

They killed Martin Luther King. They killed us.

I am afraid the root of violence is so deep in the heart and mind and manner of this society. They killed him. They killed my hope. I do not know what to say. .

This country is able to produce King but cannot preserve King. You have him, and yet you do not have him. I am sorry for you. For me. For all of us.

I prayed for him after I learned about his assassination. And then, I said to myself. You do not have to pray for him. He does not need it. You have to pray for yourself. We have to pray for ourselves.

Ray, the last time I saw him is in Geneva, at the Pacem in Terris II conference. I was up in his room in a morning, having breakfast and discussing about the situation. We had scrambled eggs and toasts and teas. I told him: "Martin, do you know something? The poor peasants in Vietnam know all about what you and I have been doing to help the poor people here and to stop the war in Vietnam. They consider you as a bodhisattva."

A bodhisattva. An enlightened being trying to work for the emancipation of other human beings. He did not say anything but I knew he was so moved by what I said.

This morning I feel comforted a little bit comforted because I remember that I did tell him so.

Ray, send me the picture in which you and I and he were together. I want to see again the expression of his face when he told me, in Summer 1966 when we met in Chicago "I feel compelled to do anything to help stop this war". He made so great an impression in me. This morning I have the impression that I can not bear the loss.

→

Handwritten note from Thich Nhat Hanh to Ray Gould, the morning after hearing of the assassination of Martin Luther King Jr.

This brief statement, made before Nhat Hanh's massive stroke in 2014, is replete with the qualities of friendship and love. At the affective level, we see that Nhat Hanh was deeply moved by King's death. Nhat Hanh's reaction to the news of King's death was not that of a dispassionate observer, but rather of someone aware of their interconnection and of the love that provides the interconnection in both the model of reality that Nhat Hanh had inherited and in the model he adopted from King: the Beloved Community. Moreover, one does not make a "deep vow" to continue a great work of someone at a great remove, but rather to continue the work of someone we love.

Anyone who has known a great love in their life knows that the measurement of that loving relationship in days marked off on a calendar is perhaps the least meaningful way to measure the relationship, if measuring ever enters the picture. The friendship of Thich Nhat Hanh and Martin Luther King Jr. in the world we access with our senses spans a short period of time— 1965 through April 4, 1968. The points of contact between the two men over that slender skein of years is equally meager: the open letter on the immolations in Vietnam, the meeting in Chicago, the Nobel Peace Prize nomination, a second meeting in Geneva, and a tiny number of errata—these constitute the historical deposit of their relationship. Yet Nhat Hanh's 2014 statement about King is suffused with the warmth of friendship and brotherhood. Further, the same statement raises the question, of one open to life's wider reaches, to the possibility of a friendship that continued through all the observable events of Nhat Hanh's life from 1968 to 2014 and beyond, silently and invisibly to all those but Nhat Hanh himself, lending support and strength.

Is there anything in Nhat Hanh's great body of work that helps us understand how he interprets the ongoing support he felt from King? Is he merely speaking metaphorically or in the field of memory (he has "always felt his support" because he holds King and his witness in memory)? Or does Nhat Hanh mean something deeper, something about the endurance of loving relationships beyond death?

The answer to that last question is yes; Nhat Hanh has left a trail of clues that points to this remarkable conclusion: he believes that because of King's spiritual stature—the fact that he was a "bodhisattva"—he continues his loving service for the world after passing from this life. It might have sufficed to argue for their friendship using just the evidence from 1965 to 1968, but another dimension, another world, announces itself if we find that their friendship continued past King's death. We may even conclude that their friendship has developed over the decades since.

The resources that apply to the two-world friendship across time of Nhat Hanh and King are these: teachings on the nature and ministrations of bodhisattvas that are found in a play Thich Nhat Hanh wrote in 1967 that explores the afterlife and a 2002 dharma teaching book about death and life: *No Death, No Fear: Comforting Wisdom for Life.* In an introduction to the play, *The Path of Return Continues the Journey,* Nhat Hanh asks his own questions about what comes after we die:

> *Who will be gone and who will stay? Where do we come from and where will we go? Are the other shore and this shore one or two? Is there a river that separates the two sides, a river that no boat can cross? Is such complete separation possible? . . . Love enables us to see things that those who are without love cannot see.*[95]

Nhat Chi Mai

Before we take a close look at Thich Nhat Hanh's extraordinary play, it will be helpful to review a chapter from Sister Chan Khong's memoir, *Learning True Love,* which describes the historical background for the play. She tells the story of a powerful young woman, Nhat Chi Mai, chronicling her journey into deeper and deeper commitment to Engaged Buddhism.

Mai, as she was called, was the youngest child in a prosperous family, and at the beginning of her involvement in the School of Youth for Social Service (SYSS), she was naïve about politics in Vietnam.[96] In Sister Chan Khong's narration, we witness Mai's transformation into a deeply committed Buddhist social worker, concerned for the welfare of the peasants with whom SYSS worked and concerned for Vietnam as a whole. In April 1967, Mai withdrew for a period of several weeks from weekly SYSS gatherings. Then, on May 14, 1967, Mai appeared, beautifully dressed, at one of the Morning of Mindfulness meetings. Mai asked Sister Chan Khong to come to Tu Nghiem Pagoda the next Tuesday morning, which was Wesak, the festival that celebrates the Buddha's birth.[97] On that following Tuesday, before she could travel to the pagoda, Sister Chan Khong learned that Mai had immolated herself in front of the pagoda. Sister Chan Khong's response was, "Sister Mai has sacrificed herself for peace."[98]

Less than two months later, on July 5, 1967, five young men, all Buddhist members of the SYSS, were abducted late at night from their dormitory, taken to the riverbank, and shot. Four of the young men died, but Ha Van Dinh, though seriously wounded, survived (the assassins believed him to be dead and left him with the bodies of the other four).[99] Dinh was able to provide an eyewitness account of the exchanges between the assassins and the SYSS workers, dialogue which Nhat Hanh would subsequently use in his play.

In December 1967, only months after the deaths of Mai and the four young men, Nhat Hanh wrote what would be his only play, *The Path of Return Continues the Journey*, later published in a collection of his essays on nonviolent social change, *Love in Action*. Strangely, this play has received no scholarly attention and has never been produced on stage.* Perhaps when the value of *The Path of Return Continues the Journey's* value is drawn out, more attention will be given to it.

The Path of Return Continues the Journey is a play of ideas, with very little action. After the four young murdered social workers join Mai in a boat she has rowed to the shore where their physical bodies are, they engage in a lively dialogue about the afterlife. This dialogue fills most of the brief play. It is a bit like Sartre's *No Exit*—though slightly more action-oriented, as they are rowing rather than sitting in a Second Empire drawing room. But as in *No Exit,* the real action is all in the thoughts expressed through the dialogue. As Sartre did in *No Exit,* Nhat Hanh uses the play to explore our inner lives and the quality of our interconnectedness, whether we are bound together by love or by violence, hatred, and ignorance. In the case of Sartre's play, the setting is a conceit; the philosopher and playwright is using the afterlife to cast light on our earthly here-and-now lives. Nhat Hanh is not at all disinterested in the phenomenal world, but in *The Path of Return Continues the Journey,* he is making a genuine attempt to speak of our continued existence after death—the ongoing lives of bodhisattvas whose mortal lives have been cut short.

The Path of Return Continues the Journey

The action of the play begins at one in the morning on July 5, soon after the murders on the banks of the Saigon River.[100] Mai, who had immolated herself less than two months earlier, rows a boat to the shore and invites the four murdered young men—Hy, Lanh, Tho, and Tuan—in their spirit bodies, to join her in the

---

* It has not been produced to my knowledge, the knowledge of the Plum Village Community in France, and the knowledge of Parallax Press, which was established by Nhat Hanh and published *Love in Action.*

boat, where they all row and engage in a wide-ranging conversation about life, death, the afterlife, and the relation between the living and the dead. What can we learn here about Nhat Hanh's beliefs concerning the afterlife, beliefs that relate to what I call the friendship he continued with King following King's own death?

First, the characters are presented as bodhisattvas. It is meaningful that Mai comes to them in a boat and that they row together. Thich Nhat Hanh is part of one of the two largest subdivisions of Buddhism, the Mahayana. *Mahayana* means "great vehicle." The vehicle is "great" because it is meant for all of life. The presence of bodhisattvas, enlightened beings who follow a vow to stay within this phenomenal world as they work, by means of compassion, to awaken all beings, distinguishes Mahayana from the other great subdivision of Buddhism, Theravada. We would expect, consistent with the metaphor of the great raft, that it is the bodhisattvas who provide the energy to move all toward enlightenment. Just so, Mai, Hy, Lanh, Tho, and Tuan are propelling the raft forward by their compassion. At one point, Mai says, "Since then [meaning her death], I have had all the time in the world, and I have been very peaceful. My heart went out to each one of you. *Many times I came to aid and protect you [my emphasis]*."[101]

Other than Mai and the four murdered SYSS workers, there are two other characters in the play, who are referred to but don't make direct appearances: Vui and Lien, two young women in the SYSS who had been murdered in a terrorist raid on the school on April 24, 1967. In the play, Mai says that Sister Vui "is still working for the villagers."[102] Tho questions this—how can she work for the villagers after having been killed? Mai replies, "Anywhere there are men and women—hell, heaven, wherever there are villages—Vui cannot *not* work for the villagers."[103]

Mai and Vui are continuing their work as bodhisattvas, and in the course of the play, we see that the four men who have just entered the afterlife are also gently being ushered into their new role as disembodied bodhisattvas. Near the end of the play, Lanh says this:

> Let us hope that our earthly lives, as well as our deaths, have sown the seeds of tolerance and love. Sister Mai's death, for instance, did not provoke any hatred. On the contrary, it awakened in many people the ability to understand and sacrifice, even people far away.[104]

In response, Mai tells them that they are approaching dawn—and the source of the river. She explains that they will be met by Vui and Lien and urges them to row a bit harder, that is, to redouble their efforts as bodhisattvas in partnership with her, Vui, and Lien, and the full shining array of bodhisattvas.

Insofar as we have already seen that Nhat Hanh regards King as a bodhisattva, the importance of this theme in the play—bodhisattvas who have had their lives cut short in a violent death, and their subsequent activity in the afterlife—is obvious. Nhat Hanh's statement that he had "always felt his [King's] support" now appears not as a piece of sentimental rhetoric, but rather as a rooted conviction, a reflective belief held by Nhat Hanh from at least the 1960s onward.

My interpretation of Thich Nhat Hanh's play is that he has cast Mai, the young Buddhist nun who had recently self-immolated, as a holy person, a bodhisattva; the four young men who had been murdered are bodhisattvas-in-the-making. Mai, I believe, is taking them on a journey of transformation, helping them to adjust to their new life as bodhisattvas, to embrace its possibilities while shedding the traces of their personal lives—their human personalities—that have bound them to the soul that normally would transmigrate. These traces, in the short interlude between the men's violent deaths and their liberation to a new life interwoven in the web of mutual causality and interconnection, they still see and believe to be real. The time of adjustment, the scope of activity, the potential for beneficent action in the afterlife, all of this is different for beings who have already advanced far along the bodhisattva path than for people still more ensnared by ordinary desires, aims, and goals. Nhat Hanh is presenting, in the play, both Mai and the young men just murdered as bodhisattvas whose mortal lives have been cut short. The young men in the raft with Mai are quickly adjusting to their new conditions, and beginning to realize their potential; they respond with joy and even playfulness.

In Nhat Hanh's play, Mai and the four SYSS workers explore not only the Saigon River but also the coves and inlets of the Buddhist afterlife. One of the intriguing ideas explored in the play that is also relevant to understanding the King–Nhat Hanh friendship after King's death has to do with the body:

> *HY: Perhaps we dead are more forgiving because we no longer have to bear the heavy burden of our bodies, and their desires and angers. Desire and anger need a home, and now that we no longer have our bodies . . .*

> *MAI: But Hy, how can you say that we no longer have our bodies? How could I see you if you didn't have a body? Our bodies are no longer heavy, no longer a burden, that's all. See how small and delicate this boat is, and yet it carries all five of us with ease.*[105]

In my reading of the play, Nhat Hanh seems to affirm the reality of a body for a person soon after death, but he says that these afterlife bodies are the result of our expectations. These bodies will drop away as we become used to life in the nexus of interconnectedness and mutual causality. More powerful than any action these temporary afterlife bodies can carry out is what can happen in this new mode of life. There remains a person in the afterlife, but a person interwoven with all that is, disembodied but not extinguished. Through the reality of interbeing—interconnection and interpenetration—the person who has died, and especially one who is committed to and lives in love (bodhisattvas), lives on as an active force in the web of intercausality.

> *THO: I see, Sister Mai! You are saying that I am present in her [his mother] now, too, and in all who love me in the world of the living. That is why I am still there, and still able to provoke this chain reaction.*

> *MAI: That's right. But you are not only present within them, you are present outside them as well. All you have said and done has already begun its journey. You are present everywhere. . . . [The dead] are even more present in the world of the living. Their presence there is clearer and more substantial than in this world.[106]*

What Thich Nhat Hanh seems to propose in the play is an unfolding awareness of the liberated existence of the bodhisattvas after death. For a short time, at least, there is an organized, discrete body that resembles the earthly one, but it is much lighter and is malleable according to the will. In the ongoing, earthly circle of life in the phenomenal realm, the beneficent influence of the bodhisattva continues under the heading of "correlated reactions."[107]

Men Are Such Pitiful Creatures

Running throughout *The Path of Return Continues the Journey* is a truth that we have seen is shared in the lineage of the Fellowship of Reconciliation's nonviolence teachings and practice—violence directed toward those who act violently against us is misplaced. Our enemies are not our enemies; when we see with love, we see that the true enemies are forces beyond those people who are oppressing and wounding us. Equally, we realize that those violent people do not see us for who we are. First, they mistake *roles* for *persons*, and, even more importantly, they fail to recognize our interconnectedness—they wound themselves when they wound us:

> TUAN: *When I was alive, not a day passed when I did not recite the Heart Sutra. I thought I understood it. But it was only when the man with the poncho pointed a gun at my head that I really saw what the Heart Sutra was all about.*
>
> LANH: *Tell us, Brother Tuan, what did you see?*
>
> TUAN: *It's hard to say, Lanh. It's not something to be understood but to be seen. We can easily explain what we understand, but not what we see or perceive. It came all of a sudden, like lightning.*
>
> LANH (begging): *But try, Brother Tuan, what did you see?*
>
> TUAN: *Well, when that man with the poncho brought his gun up to my head, I realized immediately, without being aware of it consciously, that he was not going to shoot me. He was going to shoot something else, not me. How could he shoot me without knowing who I was? Since then, I have been wondering how someone can blow the brains out of another without knowing him.*[108]

Tho, who is a comic foil in the play, then remonstrates Tuan, saying that of course the murderers knew who they were. The murderers asked them over and over if they were members of SYSS, and it was because of that confirmed identity—knowing who they were socially—that they were shot. But Mai, who is more advanced in her understanding of the bodhisattva state, says that it is indeed the Heart Sutra that is needed to shatter the misguided logic underneath Tho's (and the murderers') assumptions. If the murderers could have seen that the young men were "empty" of independent identities, and if they could have seen that the social identities they thought they saw were, in fact, veils of fear and hatred that the murderers had themselves draped over the young men, they would not have killed them. Two illusions, then, were operative: the illusion of a solid independent self and the miasma cast by fear and hatred on the true disposition of reality.

Mai continues by recounting an experience that their brother social worker Duc had shared with her. Duc had had a conversation with a young American soldier, who said his mission in Vietnam was to destroy the Viet Cong "in order to save the Vietnamese and the free world."[109] Duc asked the soldier, "Are you afraid of the Viet Cong?" a question that alarmed the American, making him think he was being threatened by one of them. The soldier began interrogating Duc, hoping to make him admit to being a Viet Cong, and the situation quickly became dangerous. By staying calm and resisting the temptation to answer the American soldier's questions flippantly, Duc was able to walk away from the encounter unharmed. Duc concluded by saying that if he had been killed by the soldier, it would not have been he himself who was killed, but the soldier's image of a Viet Cong. Mai ends by saying, "Who is really killing us? It is fear, hatred, and prejudice."[110]

Dinh, one of the five SYSS workers taken to the Saigon River to be executed, survived the attack, remarkably, and he was able to give a first-person account of the events. Nhat Hanh weaved Dinh's witness into his play and used the account to say something "true"—exposing the murderers' thoughts, which would have been opaque to us if Dinh had not survived.

Love Enables Us to See Things That Those Who Are without Love Cannot See

The revelatory power of love breaks through in several places in Nhat Hanh's play. First, in the introduction, Nhat Hanh, anticipating questions of his readers as to the veracity of what happens in the play, says that he saw "fourteen eyes looking at [him]."[111] These are the eyes of the seven characters in the play (Mai and six young SYSS workers who had been murdered, the four young men as well as the two young women, Lien and Vui, who had died some months earlier). These seven people see Nhat Hanh, and Nhat Hanh sees them, because all eight of them "see" with the faculty of love. Then he goes on to assert the following:

> *I have said that it is true because I have lived the life of the story. No scientific instrument can verify the existential nature of life in this story. Love enables us to see things that those who are without love cannot see.*[112]

As the characters continue to row, a contemplative silence in their conversation is followed by "flarebombs exploding on the river, illuminating the water":[113]

> *HY: They fire flarebombs all night, don't they?*
>
> *LANH: If they could see the dead, they would know we are rowing leisurely on the river. And they would hear the sound of the water lapping against the side of our boat in the dead of night.*
>
> *HY: They don't see us only because they don't think of us. If our beloved Brother Duc were there on the riverbank, he would see us and wave.*[114]

In the above passage, *think* surely means more than "call to mind." In my interpretation, Nhat Hanh is saying that when we remember the dead with loving thoughts, their afterlife bodies can become visible to us, as do the traces of their loving action in the phenomenal world of interdependent causality.

What can Nhat Hanh mean when he claims that he has lived the life of the story? The truth of this statement can only be grasped from a nondual perspective. Nhat Hanh knows birth and no-birth, death and no-death. And, as we shall see in the following section, for Nhat Hanh, the only Buddha is a living Buddha, the only nirvana a nirvana of the moment, of this world. Both the Buddha and nirvana are touched by cultivating the capacity for love, seeing by means of love.

Our Lives as Artists

At several points in the play, Nhat Hanh refers to art—drawing, painting, music, and poetry are mentioned. After Mai brings the four men into her boat, she tells them they are going to see their friends, Sisters Lien and Vui, who had been murdered several months earlier. Tho asks Mai how Sisters Lien and Vui occupy themselves now. Mai says that Vui is still working, but that Lien, "just takes it easy—walking, reading the Heart Sutra, giving Vui drawing lessons."[115] As the references to drawing and painting are expanded later in the play, we begin to understand that Sister Vui is teaching more than how to draw; she is teaching Lien the art of living love.

Mai says she is eager to see Sisters Lien and Vui to see how their art has been perfected in the afterlife. Mai is sure that the inspiration for their drawing now comes directly from the Heart Sutra, and she adds:

> MAI: We each paint our own lives. If your work is broad and free, your life will be broad and free, also. That is all. We create our own worlds with our visions, conceptions, and thoughts. We might create a constricted world of suffering and sorrow, or one that is immense and free, a truly beautiful place. The essential ingredient is a spirit of openness, tolerance, and freedom. . . .
>
> HY: Now I understand what Brother Tuan meant when he said, "The mind is like a painter."
>
> MAI (laughs): Yes. Why don't you all begin here and now to paint your own lives. Every artist is capable, through his art, of reaching the

supreme objective of life itself. . . . The strokes of your painting are those of love. Not only scenes of mountains or clouds or immense skies are breathtaking. Lonely pines standing on snowy cliffs can also be free and bold. The world of the bodhisattvas also has lakes and ponds, low hills, curved bridges, and red earthen paths.[116]

The meaning seems to be that the life of the bodhisattva is the life of everyday acts of love, cultivated both "outside" and "inside." The simple, even humble, cultivation of the inner landscape and of one's interactions (though the body may be elsewhere, the actions remain in the chain of mutual causality) is the art of the bodhisattva's life.

Lessons from No Death, No Fear

Thirty-five years after Nhat Hanh wrote *The Path of Return Continues the Journey*, he published the book *No Death, No Fear: Comforting Wisdom for Life*. Nhat Hanh had been living in exile, mostly in France, since 1966, and after the end of the Vietnam War, his work in supporting the Beloved Community grew and evolved. Exile blocked his ability to continue his revival and reform of Buddhism in Vietnam and Southeast Asia. More and more, he lived an engaged life grounded in the place and the moment in which he lived, and he was also working out the meaning of becoming "at home in the world."

No Death, No Fear contains teachings that will help us see how the friendship of King and Nhat Hanh continued after King's death. The book expresses Nhat Hanh's central ideas about death and the afterlife in a simpler, more prosaic way than the play does, and it usefully augments what is portrayed in the play. *No Death, No Fear* represents the fruit of more than three decades of practice and meditation since the play was written.

When you lose a loved one, you suffer. But if you know how to look deeply, you have a chance to realize that his or her nature is truly

the nature of no birth, no death. There is manifestation and there is
cessation of manifestation in order to have another manifestation.
You have to be very keen and very alert in order to recognize the
new manifestation of just one person. But with practice and with
effort you can do it.[117]

Where would we look for the manifestation of a person we
love and have lost to death? What kind of keenness and alertness
is needed? What should we practice? In *No Death, No Fear*, we
may find the clues as to how Nhat Hanh maintained his friendship with King by listening closely to his advice about death.

As before, the watchword for the effortful meditation that
allows one to see the new manifestation of a lost friend is love.
The bodhisattva of compassion, Avalokiteshvara, bases his compassion on deep listening.[118] We attend to those we love. When
the deity and great bodhisattva Avalokiteshvara attended with
love to the nature of reality, he awakened to the truth that all
beings are without separate selves—he saw into the meaning of
emptiness. "Seeing this, he overcame all his suffering."[119]

Nhat Hanh distinguishes sharply between a conceptual
notion of emptiness—that we have no separate selves—and an
experiential grasp of emptiness and, indeed, between any idea
and the reality to which it points. The notion of the Buddha is
not the living Buddha:

The Buddha said in the Ratnakuta Sutra: "If you are caught
by the notion of being and non-being, then the notion of emptiness can help you to get free. But if you are caught by the notion
of emptiness, there's no hope." The teaching on emptiness is a
tool helping you to get the real insight of emptiness, but if you
consider the tool as the insight, you just get caught in an idea.[120]

Nhat Hanh admits that we value notions and concepts that are
helpful to us, that help us understand things, and therefore, it is
difficult to let them go in order to inhabit direct reality unclouded

by symbols. Nhat Hanh goes on to explain with a metaphor of a match and a fire. The match is the notion or concept. "When you have a match, you have the condition to make a fire." You have an idea of what the fire will be. But the fire (reality itself) that is set by the match (the notion) is so much greater, fiercer, and more beautiful than the igniting match that our love moves to the fire, and the match is ultimately consumed by the resulting fire.[121]

With respect to the manifestation of Martin Luther King Jr., in order for Thich Nhat Hanh to recognize King himself rather than merely his own previously held images and notions about King, Nhat Hanh would need to use his memories, perceptions, and feelings about King to look closely at the present moment in order to discern King's continued living manifestation. Then he would inhabit the moment, with love, long enough that the notion—his memories of and ideas about King—could fall away, and King could manifest in the present. Is there any further clue as to what Thich Nhat Hanh might look for as he looks intently within and without for his friend?

I suggest that the occurrence of raising the tension would be one marker to the continuing presence of King in Nhat Hanh's life. Nhat Hanh has related that at their last meeting together, in Geneva, he told King that in Vietnam, people called King a bodhisattva for his compassion in awakening people. By drawing together King's reference to raising the tension as a gadfly in the "Letter from a Birmingham Jail," and by suggesting that King's nomination of Nhat Hanh for the 1967 Nobel Peace Prize was an international, nonviolent instance of this raising the tension, we may conclude that the particular facet of the bodhisattva that Nhat Hanh had in mind in King was this quality of rousing people from complacency and moral and spiritual slumber. King is a bodhisattva whose life, powered by compassion, cannot be stopped by the assassin's bullet.

Thich Nhat Hanh and the Beloved Community

Thich Nhat Hanh, like Muste, Thurman, and King, made several striking, important additions to our understanding of the Beloved Community. First, working within his own root-religion of Buddhism, he began to break the barriers between monastic life and the life of ordinary people. At about the same time, Nhat Hanh began his work of promoting gender equality within Buddhism. He also expanded the idea of the Beloved Community to include all of life, not just human life. The expansion of the Beloved Community was also given a time dimension by Nhat Hanh. He helped us see that the work of enlightened beings doesn't end with death—they are here with us, helping us manifest the Beloved Community. Finally, Nhat Hanh taught the world mindfulness and, in so doing, furthered the cause of universal peace and justice, the work that manifests the Beloved Community. In 2014, Nhat Hanh said that he had kept his vow to continue King's work of manifesting the Beloved Community. Let's look more closely at Nhat Hanh's contributions to this work.

The Order of Interbeing

In 1966, Nhat Hanh ordained six Vietnamese Buddhists into the Order of Interbeing (*Tiep Hien* in Vietnamese), an order inclusive of the four sectors of the full Buddhist Sangha—monks, nuns, laymen, and laywomen.[122] These six young people were the leaders of the SYSS. At their ordination, they vowed to observe the Fourteen Mindfulness Trainings of the Order of Interbeing, and to practice at least sixty Days of Mindfulness a year. Here is what Sister Chan Khong wrote about how she practiced a Day of Mindfulness while still resident and working in Vietnam:

"I so looked forward to these days. I dwelled mindfully on each act, beginning as I placed down my overnight bag in my room, boiled water to prepare a bath, and then put on my meditation clothes. First I did walking meditation alone in the woods and picked some wildflowers and bamboo branches for flower arrangements. Then after a few hours of dwelling mindfully in each act and releasing most of my worries, I began to feel renewed." After practicing sitting and walking meditation, the six members gathered together to recite the Fourteen Mindfulness Trainings and chant the Heart of the Prajñaparamita Sutra.[123]

The practice of mindful looking, the recitation of the Fourteen Mindfulness Trainings, and the chanting of the Heart Sutra all aided the members of the order in maintaining their vision of reality—a world, despite the violence all around them, that was patterned by interbeing and emptiness. For instance, the first three of the Fourteen Mindfulness Trainings all help the practitioner realize the emptiness (permeability) and thus the interconnection of structures, of "things:" Openness means training to not cling too closely to any doctrine, even core Buddhist doctrines; Non-attachment to Views teaches the practitioner to remember that there is always more to learn, that our current understanding is partial; and Freedom of Thought commits the practitioner to guarding not only one's own freedom of thought but the freedom of those in our circle, including the agency for children to develop their own views and opinions apart from that of their parents or teachers. A person practicing the first three of the Fourteen Mindfulness Trainings is enabled to better grasp that no category of being is sealed off from any and all other categories—all the categories are empty of independent being. The Order of Inter-being still continues to this day, and many people are ordained each year.

Interconnectedness—*interbeing* in Nhat Hanh's usage—is central to the understanding of the Beloved Community. Inter-being is learned in practical ways by living within the Order of Interbeing, by absorbing Nhat Hanh's teachings through his books and dharma talks, and by attending retreats at his various communities. However, Nhat Hanh in all of the previous is not only simply passing on what he received about interconnected-ness and the Beloved Community from King. In fact, Nhat Hanh possessed his own—Buddhist—understanding of interconnec-tion and community building that brings a new dimension to the lineage teaching from Royce to King and then to Nhat Hanh.

The fundamental Beloved Community concept of intercon-nectedness may be explained like this: all of us are connected, as if each of us has a cord around our waist and from that cord an innumerable set of other cords radiate outward, connecting to all other beings. Nhat Hanh brought the idea of interpenetration to that of simple interconnectedness. A lyrical way of speaking of interpenetration comes from the poet William Blake: "to see the universe in a grain of sand." Interpenetration is the insight that the whole is completely present in each of the parts of the whole. A core idea in Nhat Hanh's school of Buddhism, interpenetration is not unknown in Western thought and religion. For instance, one early Christian writer said that in each person's heart all the demons of hell and all the angels of heaven are present, and that at the center of the heart—the center of the center—Christ is enthroned; that is, the whole world is present in each human heart. For this seventh century Christian theologian, Maximus the Confessor, a human capability is taking into the self all of the cosmos by means of gazing lovingly at the world. By means of the loving gaze, the world is gathered into the person's interior. The contemplative becomes a microcosm of the universe.[124]

Interpenetration makes compassion comprehensible. Certainly, the awareness that we are connected mitigates rapaciousness—consumerism that treats other beings as senseless goods to be used. True *compassion*, however, is much more than just knowing that I'm connected to you. Self-interest alone can govern my behavior in a world that is interconnected but not perceived to be interpenetrating. *Compassion* literally means "feeling with," and my capacity to feel with you—or with a caribou, or with a dying star—stems from the reality that the caribou is calving *in me*, that the star is flinging its elements into the space around it *in me*. As the idealistic Mr. Emerson exclaims, in Forster's *A Room with a View*, in response to the issue of having a room in the hotel *with* or *without* a view: "I don't care what I see outside. My vision is within!" He continues, hitting his chest over his heart: "Here is where the birds sing! Here is where the sky is blue!"

Thich Nhat Hanh and a Creative Interplay with His Tradition

Thich Nhat Hanh not only created the Order of Interbeing and the School of Youth for Social Service—both institutions helping to erase the false barriers between the Buddhist monastic life and the life of people living "in the world"—he also wrote powerful critiques of Buddhist doctrinal interpretation that he believed distorted the full manifestation of the Beloved Community. Anything that falsely separates one being from another or falsely elevates the dignity of one being over another distorts the true manifestation of the Beloved Community. Both by critiquing errors in Buddhist doctrine and by putting forward doctrinal interpretations that show how all of life is interconnected, he helps us see the Beloved Community in its shining reality.

Thich Nhat Hanh stands at the confluence of the Buddhist traditions and lineages outlined previously. He is a scholar and acknowledged dharma teacher, having received the "lamp transmission" in the 42nd generation of the Lam Te Dhyana (Rinzai Zen in Japanese) school.[125] Nhat Hanh has actively worked with the dharma tradition he has received—reinterpreting, correcting, re-establishing, and creatively applying the rich interweaving of Buddhist thought that has flourished in Vietnam. Over his long life of writing and teaching, several central themes have emerged where his ideas are distinctive. With respect to interbeing, Nhat Hanh has critiqued long-standing commentaries on the variously numbered "links" of causation (in the following, I am paraphrasing with my own reading, not directly quoting).

First, Thich Nhat Hanh points out that various commentaries on the links of causation have, in effect, withdrawn from the full understanding of dependent co-arising and have substituted a limited, linear chain of causation. Nhat Hanh notes that these commentaries begin with what becomes, in effect, a first cause—life is suffering. Nhat Hanh rejoins that life is suffering and non-suffering. From this first mistaken link of causation, the interpretation moves forward along a single line: this formation leads to this, and so on.

Not only is the statement "life is suffering" a retraction from the fullness of interbeing, it is needlessly negative, Nhat Hanh says. The Buddha did not say that life equals suffering, but that life contains both suffering and non-suffering. Life has elements not only of pain and sadness but also of beauty and joy.

The negative and linear view of causation does not correspond with the complex nature of reality. According to this view, *Nirvana* (Sanskrit, from a root meaning "extinguished," "blown-out," as in a candle flame), becomes a goal for the future or after one has departed this phenomenal life. What is actually extinguished in Nirvana is our afflictions and "wrong view," the view that doesn't correspond with the interbeing nature of reality. However, Thich Nhat Hanh maintains that nirvana isn't something to be attained in the future, but that it is present and available, here and now, in the very midst of life.

Nirvana in this life is cultivated by two primary practices for Nhat Hanh: guarding the gateways of the senses, and "watering" the good seeds (*bija*) in the field storehouse of consciousness. For Nhat Hanh, it is quite important that we use our senses to take in compassion, love, beauty, and peace, and to exclude violence, degradation, manipulation, and other debasing modes of life. Each sense impression plants a seed in the storehouse of consciousness. Nhat Hanh recognizes that excluding all negative seeds is impossible, and that such an effort at perfection will lead one astray. Instead, mindfulness directed toward the seeds of the consciousness will water some, and withdraw attention from others, such that they do not grow. Through these twin practices of guarding the gateways of the senses and of inner gardening, nirvana may manifest in this life.

Engaged Buddhism

Every movement toward interconnection, every overcoming of barriers, whether these acts are at the most intimate level (like Nhat Hanh and King becoming friends, brothers) or at the greatest scale we can imagine (healing the relationship between humans and the planet)—each of these moves is like Nhat Hanh keeping his vow to maintain the Beloved Community. It doesn't matter if the person who makes this move is fully conscious of what the Beloved Community is—and is acting out of love for and loyalty to that community—or if the act is a simple hope to heal a breach in one's life. The effect is the same: maintaining the Beloved Community. When Nhat Hanh began creating the movement that came to be known as Engaged Buddhism, he had not yet met King. Nhat Hanh had his own worldview, one that envisioned peace among all beings and witnessed to the interconnected reality of the world.

With a vision informed by a full grasp of interbeing, the young monk saw that the Buddhist monastic life was needlessly constricted, contained within their own communities and with limited interaction with the outside world. Such withdrawal is warranted if life is seen as a negative from which one must escape. Extensive contact with the outside world was seen as contaminating. By overcoming those false barriers between monks and the rest of Vietnamese people, Nhat Hanh was maintaining the Beloved Community. Engaged Buddhism was maintaining the Beloved Community long before Nhat Hanh learned of it from King.

Traditionally Buddhist monks performed acts of charity—giving food, medicine, and money to poor people. In 1964, Thich Nhat Hanh made a formal proposal to the newly-founded Unified Buddhist Church, that they go beyond such traditional notions of charity by supporting the peasants in their efforts to improve the quality of their lives. His idea was to train a corps of young Buddhists, both lay and monastic, to learn social work and rural development techniques that support the work of personal and community transformation.[126]

Engaged Buddhism is quite simple: it is the Buddhist acting and existing in the world outside the monastery—in effect, dissolving the boundary between the world and the monastery. Here, in Thich Nhat Hanh's lucid language, is one way he describes Engaged Buddhism:

> *When you drink your tea, if you are really there, so that life, peace, happiness, and joy are possible, that is already Engaged Buddhism. When you practice in the heart of your family, your community, your city, your society, that is Engaged Buddhism. The way you walk, the way you look, the way you sit, can be very engaged, because they have an influence on the society where you live, and you inspire people to do like you, so that peace, happiness, joy, and brotherhood are possible at every moment.*

The war itself was the fuel that led Nhat Hanh to Engaged Buddhism. Witnessing the suffering of so many Vietnamese people, as well as the suffering of the creatures and the land itself stirred Nhat Hanh's compassion.

> *The term "Engaged Buddhism" was created during the time of the Vietnam War. As monks, nuns, and laypeople during the war, many of us practiced sitting and walking meditation. But we would hear the bombs falling around us, and the cries of the children and adults who were wounded. To meditate is to be aware of what is going on. What was going on around us was the suffering of many people and the destruction of life. So we were motivated by the desire to do something to relieve the suffering in us and around us.*
>
> *We wanted to serve, and we wanted to practice sitting and walking meditation to give us the stability and peace we needed to go out of the temple and help relieve this suffering. We walked mindfully right alongside suffering, in the places where people were still running under the bombs. We practiced mindful breathing as we cared for children wounded by guns or bombs. If we didn't practice while we served, we would lose ourselves, burn out, and not be able to help anyone.*
>
> *Engaged Buddhism was born from this difficult situation; we wanted to maintain our practice while responding to the suffering.*

The Buddhist leadership in Vietnam at the time was conservative and deeply suspicious, if not disapproving, of these progressive developments.[127] The ongoing war and the efforts of the Vietnamese Buddhist leadership to suppress Nhat Hanh's efforts led to a scattering and dissolution of the nascent Buddhist social work communities. Nhat Hanh himself fell sick—so sick, he later wrote, that he almost died.[128] Nevertheless, today Nhat Hanh's view of interbeing has spread around the world.[129] Engaged Buddhism, beginning with the work of Nhat Hanh, despite opposition and oppression in Vietnam, flourishes today in many countries. As Engaged Buddhism flourishes, the Beloved Community is maintained.

Thich Nhat Hanh Removes Barriers between Buddhism and Christianity

The challenges to maintaining the Beloved Community are easy to discern in our everyday world. Wherever we encounter divisions that lift some up and oppress others, we recognize the betrayal of the Beloved Community. Among the most notorious divisions of our world are those between religions. As Howard Thurman worked to include racial reconciliation in the maintenance of the Beloved Community, Nhat Hanh has helped lower the barriers between two of the great world religions, Buddhism and Christianity.

The continuing and developing friendship between King and Nhat Hanh led Nhat Hanh to further explore the relationship between Buddhism and Christianity. As he wrote in *Living Buddha, Living Christ,*

> *It was only later, through friendships with Christian men and women who truly embody the spirit and understanding and compassion of Jesus, that I have been able to touch the depths of Christianity. The moment I met Martin Luther King, Jr., I knew I was*

in the presence of a holy person. Not just his good work but his very
being was a source of great inspiration for me.[130]

The brotherhood of Nhat Hanh and King began, as we've seen, with the open letter Nhat Hanh sent to King explaining the self-immolation of Buddhist monks—that these were not suicides, as had been widely reported in the Western press, but acts of total commitment and love. It is important to remember that the self-immolations were not only, or even primarily, in protest of the war. Rather, it was the heavy-handed tactics of the American-backed Roman Catholic president of South Vietnam, Ngo Dinh Diem, against the Buddhist population that resulted in these ultimate gestures of dissent and hope. Notably, some of the first self-immolations, such as that of Thich Quang Duc, in 1963 were around Wesak, the celebration of the Buddha's birthday.

President Diem's elder brother, Ngo Dinh Thuc, was the Roman Catholic archbishop of Hue and he was allegedly party to the oppression of South Vietnamese Buddhists. On Wesak in 1963, gunshots from military police killed nine Buddhists who were protesting for religious freedom, and in the ensuing months, some four hundred Buddhists across the country were either killed or disappeared. Roman Catholics were a small minority in Vietnam before and during the Vietnam War with the United States, but this minority held disproportionate authority and power because it was tied to the colonial French government. After North Vietnam fell to communist forces and the country divided politically, about one million Roman Catholics fled the north for South Vietnam, where they became even more influential once Ngo Dinh Diem became Prime Minister and later President. President Diem issued decrees suppressing the celebration of Wesak; this oppressive move instigated the most widespread and intense protests, including the self-immolations of monks and nuns.

That it was a Roman Catholic regime that was oppressing Buddhists makes Nhat Hanh's cross-religious friendships all the more striking. Against the backdrop of the experience of Buddhists in South Vietnam in the 1950s and 1960s, the friendship of Nhat Hanh with American Christians stands out as truly remarkable.

The friendship between King and Nhat Hanh is precious for being such a shining example of the overcoming of barriers; it is a friendship that embodies the interrelated nature of reality, embodying even the Beloved Community itself. While there are good reasons for us to focus on the friendship between King and Nhat Hanh, Thich Nhat Hanh developed a circle of close friendship in the United States that also included the Cistercian monk Thomas Merton and the Jesuit priest and activist Daniel Berrigan. Looking briefly at Nhat Hanh's friendship with Merton and Berrigan provides important context and shows a bit more of the fabric of the Beloved Community as Nhat Hanh has experienced it. Nhat Hanh has written that love leads us to be deeply attentive to the lives of those we love, to explore their worlds with care and deep looking and listening.[131]

Thomas Merton was a Cistercian monk and author. His 1948 autobiography, *The Seven Storey Mountain,* made him famous, and its powerful prose pulled scores of young American men into Catholic seminaries and monasteries. But the model of the Roman Catholic priesthood the book espoused was world-denying,* and by the 1960s, a different Merton had emerged, one who did not shun the world, who advocated nonviolent action against the Vietnam War.

---

* In 2015, I met American Catholic author James Carroll at a gathering following the graduation ceremony of the Church Divinity School of the Pacific in Berkeley and asked him about *The Seven Storey Mountain.* He described it as a "deeply dangerous book" because of that world-denying position.

It was in the context of peace activism that Merton and Nhat Hanh met. Jim Forest, a former officer with the Fellowship of Reconciliation, and friend of both Nhat Hanh and Merton, has written that they met only once, at Gethsemani Abbey, Merton's monastic home in Kentucky, in May 1966 (Nhat Hanh and King would meet just weeks later, in June).[132] As with the brief encounters between King and Nhat Hanh, however, this meeting was full of significance. Merton subsequently wrote a seminal interreligious essay, "Nhat Hanh Is My Brother":

> *Thich Nhat Hanh . . . is my brother. He is more my brother than many who are nearer to me by race and nationality, because he and I see things exactly the same way. He and I deplore the war that is ravaging his country. We deplore it for exactly the same reasons: human reasons, reasons of sanity, justice and love. . . .*
>
> *I have said that Nhat Hanh is my brother, and it is true. We are both monks, and we have lived the monastic life about the same number of years. We are both poets, we are both existentialists. I have far more in common with Nhat Hanh than I have with many Americans, and I do not hesitate to say it. It is vitally important that such bonds be admitted. They are the bonds of a new solidarity and a new brotherhood that is beginning to be evident on all the five continents and that cuts across all political, religious and cultural lines to unite young men and women in every country in something that is more concrete than an ideal and more alive than a program. This unity of the young is the only hope of the world.[133]*

The entire essay is worthy of deep study, but for our purposes we can observe in it both the ideals of friendship and get a feel for what Royce and King called the Beloved Community.

Soberingly, Nhat Hanh and Merton had planned to meet again in April of 1968, at a retreat at Gethsemani Abbey that would also have included King and Vincent Harding. The retreat, however, was never to be, for it was prevented by King's assassination.

April 4, 1968, is also a connection point between Nhat Hanh and Fr. Daniel Berrigan. On that afternoon, Berrigan was the celebrant at a Eucharist held in the Columbia University rooms of David Steindl-Rast,* most likely in the rooms of the Center for Spiritual Studies that Steindl-Rast founded that year. During the Eucharist, Nhat Hanh read the Heart Sutra as one of the sacred readings. Even today such a fully interfaith Eucharist— one of the two primary sacramental rites of Christianity—is not very common. In 1968 to have a Buddhist read one of his own sacred texts within a Eucharist service would have been truly radical. After the rite was completed, all of those present left to attend a lecture by theologian Hans Kung. The lecture was interrupted by the announcement of King's murder.[134]

In 1975, Berrigan and Nhat Hanh published a set of conversations they had about Buddhism and Christianity, titled *The Raft Is Not the Shore*. In her foreword to the book, bell hooks writes that *The Raft Is Not the Shore* makes her list of books she cannot live without. There are numbers of individual statements in the book that have their own, free-standing quality, like this one that hooks quotes as a favorite: "The bridge of illusion must be brought down before a real bridge can be constructed over which human beings can pass to and from reality."[135] But it is the quality of the conversation—the mutual inquiry and spirit of respect—that catches my attention; this book reads like a dialogue between friends.

That Berrigan and Nhat Hanh were friends is borne out by private correspondence from Nhat Hanh to Berrigan that was

---

* Brother David Steindl-Rast is a leading Roman Catholic writer on contemplation. Brother David was sent by his abbot to participate in Buddhist-Christian dialogue, for which he received Vatican approval in 1967. His Zen teachers were Hakuun Yasutani Roshi, Soen Nakagawa Roshi, Shunryu Suzuki Roshi, and Eido Shimano Roshi.

shared with me by an Episcopal clergyperson who had been a confidant and friend of Berrigan. The letter, dated May 2010, was actually written by a Buddhist brother of Nhat Hanh at Nhat Hanh's request—he had asked this fellow monk to transcribe a dream he had had and send it to a friend of the community, to be conveyed with "birthday greetings and gratitude." I quote the letter somewhat extensively, as it is a unique witness to the spiritual quality of friendship that we are exploring in this chapter:

Just recently, about ten days ago, in a dream Thay saw his friend, Father Daniel Berrigan. He is now over 90 years old. Sitting next to this courageous monk [Berrigan], Thay recognized that he was worthy of all respect and reverence, even though he did not have the outer form of a Buddhist Most Venerable. Thay suggested that the community touched the earth before him. Before the community could do so, suddenly Thay saw that he was sitting alone with Father Berrigan in an open space, and he opened his arms to embrace Thay. Thay also opened his arms to embrace his friend with all his heart in the true spirit of the Plum Village practice of hugging meditation. At first, there was only happiness and the peace of brotherhood, but soon an unsettled energy arose in Thay. It was the energy of sadness, pain and loneliness. It felt strange, but Thay was able to recognize and accept these mental formations. Thay had thought that those mental formations had already been transformed, and if their energy still existed, it would be minimal.

But it was not so. Thay's whole being quaked with the feeling. Thay's arms were transmitting to the person he was embracing the energy of sadness, pain and loneliness. Thay felt clearly that the other person was also receiving it and responding to it. The time of [their] embrace was quite long, and Thay allowed himself to express those pains naturally and sincerely. Waking up, Thay knew the dream had helped his own wellbeing, because he'd had the opportunity to recognize and share his sadness and pain with a dear friend who had the capacity to touch and understand that

sadness and pain, having gone through similar difficulties, sad-
ness and loneliness. Thay thinks that in our lives, those with whom
we can share like that are few, even within our own tradition.
When we embrace a brother, a sister, a friend or a disciple, we only
want to transmit the energy of peace and love, and the other person
may believe that we only have such beautiful and peaceful energy.
But we are still human, and even though the energy of sadness
and pain may be under control and transformed, it is still there in
our human nature. If it would sleep quietly, we would be peaceful
enough. But its presence is also very important. Thanks to it, we can
recognize and understand other people's suffering and pain, and we
also can acknowledge the good fortunes and wonders available in
the present moment in us and around us.[136]

Nhat Hanh clearly had a close, intimate circle of American Christian friends, most notably King, Merton, and Berrigan. Such conscious networks of friendship "light up," as it were, parts of the all-encompassing Beloved Community, as if a small part of the entire community were to lift up out of the clouds and into clear sunlight. It is when consciousness is illuminated by love that we see intimations of the Beloved Community in its fullness. Nhat Hanh identified these three men as the source of the courage he found to explore Christianity.

Though Nhat Hanh was friends with a number of Christians, his friendship with King had unique qualities. Both Nhat Hanh and King employed the idea of the interrelated structure of reality to further their peace and justice work, and their friendship became an embodiment of this interrelatedness. Moreover, as has been mentioned earlier, Nhat Hanh called King a "bodhisattva," a title he bestowed on several other beings—Sun, Earth, the mother of Gautama Buddha, and Sister Chan Khong. Nhat Hanh, as we have learned, believes that bodhisattvas continue in some form in the afterlife, and it was because of this that his friendship with King continued to develop in the decades after King's assassination. It is this designation, "bodhisattva," that sets the friendship between King and Nhat Hanh apart from his friendships with Merton and Berrigan, though they were close and important friends.

Nevertheless, Nhat Hanh's wider circle of Christian friends, and his two books that advance Christian-Buddhist understanding—*Going Home: Jesus and Buddha as Brothers*, and *Living Buddha, Living Christ*—together have helped cross barriers between two of the world's great religions. As the barriers between people and their institutions (such as religions) come down, the doors to the Beloved Community are seen to be standing open.

Thich Nhat Hanh and Gender Equality

In today's world, we are inspired by the courage and bravery of women, often young women, leading nonviolent protests around the world, such as against the military regime's control of the government in Myanmar. The Buddhist hierarchy of Myanmar is allied with the military regime and reinforces widespread misogyny. Misogyny is embedded in cultures and religions worldwide. Nearly two billion people make up the world's two largest Christian denominations—denominations that still do not ordain women. The leadership of these denominations is held entirely by men. Out of the nearly two-thousand-year history of Christianity, women have been allowed to share in ordained ministry in some other denominations only since just before World War II.

Christianity is far from alone in institutionalizing misogyny, expressed in part by excluding women from ordained ministry and religious leadership. For instance, in 2003, in Thailand, Abbess Dhammananda became the first Thai woman to ordain as a nun in Theravada Buddhism. "Her decision sent shockwaves through the deeply conservative Thai Sangha Council, which explicitly banned the ordination of women in 1928."[137]

Extraordinarily, Nhat Hanh began ordaining women in Vietnam in the mid-1960s into the Order of Interbeing, breaking overwhelming and long-standing norms, and he continued this practice after his exile in 1966. In 1988, he performed his first monastic ordination, which included women; Sister Chan Khong became his first fully ordained monastic disciple, monk or nun. When I visited Vietnam for research on this book, I primarily interacted with the community of nuns that lives in tandem with the much-older monastic community of men where Nhat Hanh was ordained at age sixteen, and where he lives now. Nhat Hanh's longest-term colleague in leading the communities he has founded is Sister Chan Khong, whom Nhat Hanh has called a "great bodhisattva." When Nhat Hanh calls a being a "bodhisattva," he is not only voicing his belief, he is helping us see the full reaches of the Beloved Community. The Beloved Community is not a community of men alone—who, after all, make up a little less than half of the world's human population— it is men and women together, in equality. Nhat Hanh has helped Buddhism and, through Buddhism, all of us see this.

The Beloved Community Includes All of Life

Nhat Hanh has called two mortal women (as distinct from great feminine spiritual beings, like Kuan Yin) bodhisattvas—Sister Chan Khong and the mother of Gautama Buddha. Nhat Hanh called a non-Buddhist, in fact a Christian minister, a bodhisattva (King!). We might well think that when Nhat Hanh identifies a bodhisattva he is not only speaking the truth as he sees it, but expanding our vision too. So, when Nhat Hanh calls the Sun and the Earth bodhisattvas, we should pause and seek to understand the implications of these designations.

Mythologies from all times and across the world have recognized the Earth and the Sun as divinities, but how does that
make sense today with our modern science? First, the advances
of science have been in tandem with cultural shifts that have
denied the consciousness, the life, of the planet and of cosmic
bodies like the Sun. However, the demotion of the Earth's status
as a living being has more to do with economic convenience than
with science. It is easier to exploit the planet's "resources" if they
do not have the dignity and standing of beings among beings.
Tragically, this denial of status has been applied to humans as
well. Slavery is at root a denial of the status and dignity of human
beings so that those humans, who breathe, grow, live, die, think,
hope, dream, suffer, and rejoice in exactly the same ways as their
overlords do, can be used ruthlessly for economic aggrandize-
ment and luxury.

Increasingly the world is seeing the injustice and untruth of
worldviews that deny the humanity of whole swaths of the global
human population. What, then, of the planet itself and all life on
the planet? Do we have any genuine justification for denying the
consciousness, the dignity of being, of the Earth, the Sun, and all
of the cosmos? Nhat Hanh, by naming the Earth and the Sun
as bodhisattvas, challenges this prevailing perception that cannot
recognize the true status of these great beings.

In 2012, Nhat Hanh published his lyrical, stirring *Love Letter
to the Earth*. In this book, Nhat Hanh not only calls Earth a
great bodhisattva, he addresses the Earth directly as "Mother."
He goes on to diagnose many of the ills we humans suffer as
stemming from our failure to see the Earth as our mother:

> *Many of us humans, deluded by greed, pride, and delusion, have
> been unable to recognize you as our Mother. That is why we have
> caused so much suffering to one another and have damaged your
> health and your beauty.*

Nhat Hanh goes on to say that the converse of the previous is also true—that forming a right relationship to the Earth is healing and energizing:

Your immeasurable patience and endurance has made you a great bodhisattva, a solid place of refuge for us all. Every time we are unstable, every time we lose ourselves in forgetfulness, sadness, hatred, or despair, we feel the need to go back to you and practice touching the Earth. Touching you we find a refuge; we reestablish our peace, regaining our joy and self-confidence.

What Nhat Hanh says about the Earth as a whole he also believes about each being on or of the Earth—all are part of the Beloved Community. Each being, no matter how small or seemingly insignificant, shares citizenship in the Beloved Community with us. The place of each being in the Beloved Community may not stretch your mind—people today are increasingly recognizing the rights and personhood of other-than-human beings. But it would challenge many people—the kind who would agree with statements like "Fish [or any kind of animal] don't have feelings [or intelligence, or a soul], so it is okay for us to use them as food." Buddhist doctrine teaches that "all sentient beings are enlightened," but are *all* the beings of the Earth sentient? What about plants? What about rocks?

There is a famous story in the line of Buddhist teaching and practice of which Nhat Hanh is a part that tells of an early Chinese Buddhist practitioner, Daosheng. The story takes place in a time when not all the Buddhist sutras had been transmitted from India to China, so the fullness of the Buddha's teaching was not yet known. Daosheng, however, had come to a deeper understanding through practice alone, without reading or hearing all of the the sutras. Daosheng told his brother monks that all beings—including non-believers and also non-humans—had Buddhanature. The community of monks expelled Daosheng.

But one day, as two from that community were walking along a path through a mountainous area, they heard, beyond the rock wall on one side of the path, a voice speaking. The monks turned to see what was going on, and there they saw their former companion, Daosheng, preaching to the rocks—and the rocks nodding in agreement!

Cosmologist Brian Swimme and his late teacher and collaborator, Thomas Berry, write about the ancient star whose explosion as a supernova flung the essential elements that make up our solar system and comprise the elements necessary for life on this planet. They name this ancient star Tiamat and say that it sacrificed itself for our benefit. Is this merely fanciful language? Or does it convey a truth that accords with Nhat Hanh's insights about the Earth and all its component beings, as well as the Sun and the cosmos as a whole? This question can't be settled here—or even explored adequately. Consider this, however: If we treated each part of the world with the respect we give to those we recognize as our equals in everyday life, how would our behavior change? Rapaciousness would be curbed, and the Earth and all life would be protected and sustained. This healthy relationship with the Earth is the result of Nhat Hanh's expansion of the understanding of the Beloved Community to include all life, all beings.

What is the practical consequence of Nhat Hanh holding that the Beloved Community contains all of life? With the support of the Fellowship of Reconciliation, in 1970, Nhat Hanh founded Dai Dong, a Buddhist movement for the health of the Earth. Bringing together thousands of scientists and policy makers, a Dai Dong statement was signed and taken to talks with the secretary general of the United Nations, U Thant. The impact was significant and remains with us today: the first United Nations climate summit grew directly out of the conversations between Nhat Hanh and U Thant. Held in Stockholm in 1972 and called the First Earth Summit, this child of Dai Dong's interventions was the first in the great series of UN climate summits, including Kyoto, Rio, and Paris. The UN climate summit planned for November 2021 has been called by Secretary John Kerry of the United States the "last, best chance for the planet." Nhat Hanh's efforts on behalf of the great bodhisattva the Earth have helped foster a recognition of the Earth as an integral part of the Beloved Community.

Mindfulness and the Maintenance of the Beloved Community

By the time Nhat Hanh made his revelatory statement about his vow to maintain the Beloved Community in 2014, it had been almost fifty years since King's assassination. We've just looked at some of the ways that Nhat Hanh expanded the idea of the Beloved Community in that time—working to promote gender equality, to erase the false boundaries between Buddhist monastics and laypeople, to lead Buddhist monastics into loving service in the world, and to further a global environmental effort that teaches respect for all life. During those decades since 1968, however, it is teaching mindfulness that has occupied much of Nhat Hanh's energy. What if Nhat Hanh was thinking of this central work—teaching the world mindfulness—when he said he had kept his vow to maintain the Beloved Community?

It is often said that Thich Nhat Hanh has over one hundred books to his name. Most of those books deal with aspects of the inner life, of mindfulness: coping with anger or fear, finding peace and love. One of his titles is simple and direct—*The Miracle of Mindfulness*. When he is often named, along with the Dalai Lama, as one of the most famous Buddhist teachers and leaders alive today, it is largely because of his tireless teaching of mindfulness. The very centrality of mindfulness in Thich Nhat Hanh's teaching and practice would cause us to suspect that mindfulness teaching is one way he kept his vow to maintain the Beloved Community. But what a surprising idea, from an action-oriented point of view: what we cultivate in our inner lives is maintaining the Beloved Community!

If we examine Nhat Hanh's teachings on mindfulness, two main concepts stand out as helping to maintain the Beloved Community. First, mindfulness gives us the direct experience of interbeing, what King called the "interrelated structure of reality." A famous simile that Nhat Hanh has used many times is of the wave and the water. In ordinary life, I may perceive myself to be fundamentally a wave, one swell of water distinct in time and shape from all other waves. My individuality is primary. But by practicing mindfulness, I can, at any moment, "touch the ultimate," experience the ocean from which the wave arises, to which it is always connected, of which it is a part. By practicing mindfulness, I understand that my individuality is not erased and that it is truly connected to all other individuals through the encompassing ocean of being.

Another way that mindfulness maintains the Beloved Community is by rooting all our direct action in the world in an inner cultivation of nonviolence and peace. We might remember King's explanation of the three steps that must precede direct action in any nonviolent campaign, which he shared in the "Letter from a Birmingham Jail"—determining whether injustices are present, negotiation, and "self-purification." His emphasis in those steps is on self-purification: "We . . . repeatedly asked ourselves the questions 'Are you able to accept blows without retaliating?' Are you able to endure the ordeals of jail?'" The Birmingham Campaign and its related Children's Campaign can be said to have begun in the hearts of the planners, as they nurtured inner peace and nonviolence before moving into outward action.

Nhat Hanh uses a gardening metaphor to talk about the same inner process that King called *self-purification*, as a part of mindfulness. He recommends that we limit the negative messages that we allow into our consciousness from outside sources—images and messages of violence and exploitation—which he likens to the seeds of noxious weeds. Inevitably, though, such seeds do find their ways into the fields of the mind, and there they take root and begin to grow. When we perceive such choking weeds in our mind, we are at a decisive point. The temptation is to pull them out. But ripping the weeds out or chopping them down with a hoe are in themselves acts of violence—acts of violence against, we can easily see, ourselves. Nhat Hanh recommends instead that we turn our attention to nurturing the seeds of peace and compassion.

Jesus of Nazareth, whom Nhat Hanh learned to love as a brother, taught something remarkably like Nhat Hanh's mindfulness practices of ignoring the weeds and nurturing the good plants (Matthew 13:24–30):

The kingdom of heaven may be compared to someone who sowed good seed in his field; but while everybody was asleep, an enemy came and sowed weeds among the wheat, and then went away. So when the plants came up and bore grain, then the weeds appeared as well. And the slaves of the householder came and said to him, "Master, did you not sow good seed in your field? Where, then, did these weeds come from?" He answered, "An enemy has done this." The slaves said to him, "Then do you want us to go and gather them?" But he replied, "No; for in gathering the weeds you would uproot the wheat along with them. Let both of them grow together until the harvest; and at harvest time I will tell the reapers, 'Collect the weeds first and bind them in bundles to be burned, but gather the wheat into my barn.'"

From the teaching of Jesus two thousand years ago, through Martin Luther King Jr.'s self-purification in the civil rights movement, to the mindfulness of Thich Nhat Hanh, we see a rich history of the inner dimension of nonviolent action. Thich Nhat Hanh has made a monumental contribution to our understanding of the Beloved Community by opening up its inner dimensions. Further, because of the enormous reach of Nhat Hanh's teaching, millions of people have been joining Nhat Hanh in the work of maintaining the Beloved Community, all anonymously and many unaware of what the Beloved Community is. But all these people may become conscious participants in the maintenance of the Beloved Community, beyond the bounds of any world religion, King's Christianity, Nhat Hanh's Buddhism, or any other.

Thich and the Leadership of the Beloved Community

Maitreya Buddha is the next great Buddha who will manifest on the Earth, following Gautama Buddha. The word *maitreya* means "loving-kindness" in Sanskrit; Maitreya is the Buddha of love. Nhat Hanh has speculated that Maitreya Buddha will not appear as an individual person, but as the great Sangha, the spiritual community, which in Christianity we might call the community of the faithful.[138] Is it believable that Nhat Hanh, who has taken and kept a deep vow to the Beloved Community, imagines this great Sangha to be populated only by Buddhists? Pointedly, could the Sangha—as Maitreya—*not* include the bodhisattva Martin Luther King, his Christian friend? Rather, does not the Buddha of Love, composed of a luminous, universal community of bodhisattvas, seem like the Beloved Community?

Thich Nhat Hanh is preparing for this eschatological moment, the appearance of Maitreya Buddha as the Beloved Community. He has said that with his death, there will be no single leader for the Plum Village community, the tradition he has founded and currently leads. Such a move will be, no doubt, challenging for his communities. We have, I believe, a deep-seated bias in favor of the monarch/city complex. Though humans have been on the planet for many millennia (anatomically modern humans for about two hundred thousand years), human *history* is generally considered coterminous with the advent of cities, a period of around ten thousand years. Thus, for the entire stretch of written narratives we have known cities, nations, states, and the rulers of these human formations have generally been kings and emperors. It is a transformation of the highest order to move to a leaderless system.* For a world so deeply patterned by hierarchy, this transformation to a completely dispersed system of leadership will take conscious application.

Thich Nhat Hanh and the Healing of Those Who Have Died

After his exile in 1966, Nhat Hanh did not return to Vietnam until 2005. He went again in 2007 and 2008 and then moved back to his root temple, Tu Hieu, in 2018. For the 2007 visit, Nhat Hanh made several requests of the Vietnamese government, who had already enumerated conditions around the famous monk's return. Among Nhat Hanh's requests was that of holding three services, in the south, middle, and north of the country, for the recognition of those who had died in the Vietnam War, but whose bodies were never recovered. We may easily see these proposed services as acts of reconciliation and the related, subsequent healing of the Beloved Community. The services also came to be understood as reconciliation and healing for all those who had died and suffered in the war. What follows comes from

---

* There is a significant parallel between Nhat Hanh's belief that the Maitreya Buddha will appear not as an individual but as a collective—the Sangha—and the fact that the other greatest Buddhist teacher and leader alive today (in addition to Nhat Hanh) the Dalai Lama, has decided not to reincarnate after the end of this incarnation.

interviews I conducted with nuns and monks at Tu Hieu, in Hue, Vietnam, in June 2019.

My journey to Vietnam in 2019 followed an intuition. While in Hue, members of his community had told me that they did not see Nhat Hanh's return to his homeland in 2018 in the way that many had characterized it—going home to die—but I couldn't get a clear sense of what his motives were. Nhat Hanh was deeply debilitated after his stroke in 2014; he cannot talk, walk, or write. It was hard to imagine what he intended other than a peaceful time in his beloved homeland before his death.

Sister Chan Khong and some other monks and nuns who had been with Nhat Hanh in France moved to Hue with Nhat Hanh. Through my research, I had come to have high respect for Sister Chan Khong and hoped to meet and interview her and others of Nhat Hanh's community. It was from her and others in the circle of Nhat Hanh's closest living associates there in Hue that I learned about the 2007 services of reconciliation and healing that Nhat Hanh led in Vietnam.

At first, Nhat Hanh's request for the services of recognition and healing for those who had died in the Vietnam War was opposed by a variety of people and for different reasons. Those who had been allied with the North did not want people honored whom the North had considered to be American allies and enemies of the people. The same distrust was felt by South Vietnamese toward those from the North. What the two sides had in common was loss, the unfinished grieving experienced when their loved ones simply disappeared: Where were their bodies? How did they die? Who killed them? Finally, though, despite this opposition, the government and the government-sanctioned Buddhist Church permitted the services.

Many surprising things began happening upon the announcement of the services. First, the response by the Vietnamese people was overwhelming: thousands of people registered their intention to attend the services. It seemed that Nhat Hanh had discerned the need for healing among the Vietnamese people in the aftermath of a war that had been concluded some thirty-two years earlier. Beyond the response by people in all regions of the country, manifestations of the spiritual were reported.

Nhat Hanh and those helping him from Paris and elsewhere in his dispersed communities had reached an agreement with a prominent Buddhist temple in Hanoi to host the service. One woman, whose husband had disappeared during the war, decided she would attend the service in Hanoi. Weeks before the service, the woman, who had never dreamed of her husband since his disappearance, had a vivid dream in which he spoke to her and told her to attend the service, but in a location she had never heard of. When Nhat Hanh and his team arrived in Hanoi for the service, they were met with an unexpected message—the service could not be held in the temple as planned, and nowhere else in Hanoi. One of the people with Nhat Hanh had connections with a temple in a small, obscure hill village some kilometers outside of Hanoi. The decision was made to move the service there. When people began arriving in Hanoi for the service they were directed to the new location. The woman whose husband had appeared to her in a dream was astonished to hear the name of the new location—it was the one she had heard in her dream.

There was also a common experience, in all three cities where the services were held, of people seeing the spirits of their lost loved ones rising up over the scroll that listed all the disappeared, as their particular names were read.

Finally, in Vietnam in 2019, I met a young man who was born after the war. He went to one of the services as a layperson and was so moved that he was drawn to become a novice at Plum Village, Nhat Hanh's community in France. He was ordained, became one of Nhat Hanh's main attendants, and moved back to Vietnam with him.

While it might be tempting to dismiss these accounts as fanciful, looking through the lens of the Beloved Community, these experiences seem instead to be both quite powerful and meaningful. In all of the previous, there are several things revealed about Nhat Hanh and the Beloved Community. First, the embodiment of the Beloved Community in the friendship between Nhat Hanh and King is not unique, but a general feature of the interconnected, holistic model. The interconnectedness of the world is enduring and encompassing, and it transcends ordinarily perceived boundaries of time and death. As we should expect in a world that is deeply interconnected and interpenetrating, the acts of healing and growth extend both from the dead to the living and from the living to the dead. And finally, the Beloved Community itself—active and growing, of divine origin—acts to raise the consciousness of people, alerting them to the possibility of loyalty to a supernal, holistic reality.

Conclusion:
A Genuine Civilization Struggling to Be Born

King named the moment in which he was delivering his Nobel Peace Prize acceptance speech as " . . . the birth pangs of a genuine civilization struggling to be born." This statement, set against the backdrop of the sorrows he had witnessed and experienced in 1963 and 1964, up to the time of the speech in Oslo, is stunning and immediately raises some questions: How did he have the faith to liken his time to the travail of birth, and when did he expect the genuine civilization being born to appear? Let's take the second of these questions first.

Strategic and careful as King was in his planning for nonviolent action, the successes the movement was experiencing, intermixed though they were with the experiences of terror and pain, must have been heady. The March on Washington (1963) drew some quarter of a million people in front of the Lincoln Memorial; the Nobel Prize itself affirmed the movement on an international scale; and the legislative victories of the Civil Rights Act (1964) and the Voting Rights Act (1965) capped all that came before. King may well have believed that his vision of the birth of a genuine civilization (the Beloved Community) was to be filled imminently.

However, when King went to Jamaica for two months in early 1967 and wrote the first draft of what would be his final book, *Where Do We Go from Here: Chaos or Community?*, the very title of the book speaks of uncertainty. In the first chapter of the book, titled "Where Are We?," King chronicles the dispiriting chain of events that followed on the heels of the victory of the 1965 Voting Rights Act: thousands of jeering anti-protestors rained rocks and taunts down on civil rights marchers in Chicago; white and Black civil rights activists had been murdered in Southern states, and their accused murderers given easy acquittal; and Ramparts magazine had declared that " . . . the Movement is in despair because it has been forced to recognize the Negro revolution as a myth." It is doubtful that King, in early 1967, was still viewing the shadowy events of the day as birth pangs of the Beloved Community.

The closing years of the twentieth century and the first decade of this century saw several visionary thinkers begin to write and speak about a shift in consciousness that they discerned was beginning. Joanna Macy and David Korten, working separately, called this shift the Great Turning. Thomas Berry, Mary Evelyn Tucker, and Brian Swimme, working from a base of a retold universal history, also predicted the dawn of a new planetary consciousness and related civilization. Ewert Cousins and Karen Armstrong, among others, wrote of a Second Axial Age and described that new epoch in terms congruent with the language used by these other thinkers.[139]

King and Nhat Hanh forged their friendship, as we have seen, in the midst of a budding re-appreciation of life as interconnected and interpenetrating. Preaching and teaching the interrelated structure of reality; using interconnectedness as a principle in scientific and philosophical innovation; and, at the highest level, embodying the Beloved Community, as Nhat Hanh and

King did—these were the mid-century answers to the dominant model of a machine universe.

The flowering of interbeing and of holistic models of reality in the 1960s matured into the full expressions of hope such as the Great Turning and the Second Axial Age around the millennium shift in 2000. The various expressions in the 1960s of a new regard for the importance of interdependence created a fertile interplay of thought and practice. General systems theory and the Buddhist doctrine of mutual causality, for instance, together influenced Joanna Macy, and resulted in her own perception of the moment of opportunity in which we find ourselves now, which Macy and others call the Great Turning. Macy stirringly describes the grace inherent in this moment in this way:

> *To us is granted the privilege of being on hand: to take part, if we choose, in the Great Turning to a just and sustainable society. We can let life work through us, enlisting all our strength, wisdom, and courage, so that life itself can continue.*[140]

Here is how Macy describes the Great Turning itself:

> *Now, I suggest, the cognitive shifts and spiritual openings taking place in our own time can be seen as the third Turning of the Wheel, a dramatic re-emergence of the Dharma of dependent co-arising. The recognition of our essential non-separateness from the world, beyond the shaky walls erected by our fear and greed, is a gift occurring in countless lives in every generation. Yet there are historical moments when this recognition breaks through on a more collective level. This is happening now in ways that converge to bring into question the very foundation and direction of our civilization. A global revolution is occurring that is of such magnitude that people unacquainted with Buddhism are using a similar term. Many are calling it the Great Turning.*[141]

At the heart of Macy's vision, as we can see, is the recognition of the interconnectedness and interpenetration—the interbeing—of all life.

Making the connection between the interbeing and holism flowering of the 1960s and the speculation about a Second Axial Age around the time of the millennium shift is important. The contemporary expression of what might be called the "mechanistic model of the world"—or "a reductionist, atomistic model of life" or "a world marked by extreme alienation and objectification"—was the result of tributary movements flowing together over a period of centuries. Some scholars have placed the inception of the objectifying, mechanistic model of world at the end of the Medieval period,[142] so it is clear that this dominant model of the world, with its disastrous consequences, didn't appear suddenly. We should also not expect an alternate, healthier model to gain currency overnight. If King was right, if what he discerned in 1964 was producing something new and hopeful, then we might link his vision to that of Macy and others and see the dawn of the Second Axial Age as the culmination of something intuited and initiated some forty years earlier. Half a century is not too long to emerge from the shadows of an edifice built over half a millennium.

We can remember two features of the prevailing model of world civilization that predate and underlie the industrial, mechanistic model: patriarchy and hierarchy. Understanding the industrial, mechanistic model to be embedded in the vastly older and completely pervasive patriarchal-hierarchical model helps us understand the enormity of the shift necessary in the healing of the Beloved Community. The dominant model has almost unimaginably deep roots in human consciousness.

Of course, part of the slow—sometimes faltering and unsteady—growth of the Beloved Community consciousness is due to the power of the response of those who are immersed in, beholden to, and supportive of the dominant model. Of late, terms like the Great Dying and the Great Unraveling have been appearing in circles that have hoped for the Great Turning and the Second Axial Age.[143] This more negative view comes from the experiences of the front edges of the climate chaos that is, and will continue to, accompany unchecked carbon emissions, coupled with environmental degradation, the new rise of nationalism worldwide, xenophobia and associated violence toward immigrants, and racism—the persistence of which King predicted. Altogether, many feel that hope in a planetary shift toward a healthy, holistic, interconnected model was premature at best, or illusory.

How can we account for King's initial hope for the manifestation of the Beloved Community (the genuine civilization he saw being born)? What we've learned about the Beloved Community points to something other than the human subject reading the objective signs scattered in the environment around and outside of him or herself. Instead, the Beloved Community works in a coordinated fashion, the whole operating fully in each of the parts of the whole. Thus, if agape love is coursing through the universe, King could find it coursing through himself too; the signs of hope were within him.

I once heard cosmologist Brian Swimme express the same reality—the whole being present and working through all the parts of the whole—with respect to another of the forces of the universe: gravity. Swimme is a lyrical writer, able to work adroitly with both mathematical equations and the elements of language, and he talks about gravity in terms of "desire." Elements of the universe—planets, star systems, whole galaxies, desire one another, and this desire pulls them toward each other. Swimme said, "The whole universe is shot through with libido. How do

I know this? Because I am too." Laughter filled the room when Swimme said this, and he loves to teach by disarming through humor, but his point about the interrelated structure of reality was entirely substantive.

What is true of desire is true of overflowing love (agape): King could feel this most enduring, powerful force at work within himself as well as in the world around him. Inside King, the Beloved Community was being born, and we can believe he observed its advent there.

The presence of overflowing love in King and in Nhat Hanh is a protecting and transforming power. In a recent conversation I had with veteran civil rights activist Ruby Sales, she said that she has come to believe that learning to love ourselves is key to not only individual health but to the health of communities and even nations. If we have vacated our souls, or deadened ourselves to our inner lives, and do not know them to be bursting with agape love, then we can be manipulated, and we will act on the orders of others. "Why would you let yourself be a foot soldier in someone else's war," Ruby asked, and then gave her own answer, "Because by not loving ourselves we have committed 'soul murder.'"

Although this may sound grim and judgmental to you, perhaps you can use the need for loving yourself as the place to locate your lever that begins to move the outgrown model of the world that is dragging all of life down. I am reminded of one of the New Testament stories of Jesus, the story of the woman with a flow of blood. She had had this hemorrhage for a dozen years, and had exhausted her finances on cures that left her worse off in the end (there is a Sam Cooke song that beautifully tells this little story of Jesus so compellingly, "Touch the Hem of His Garment"). She had heard about Jesus, who had just arrived in her region. She joined a tremendous crowd that was pressing around and jostling Jesus, seeking his healing.

One detail of this little story is essential for grasping its power and how it applies to King, Nhat Hanh, and us. A woman menstruating in Jesus's culture was ritually unclean, and to touch an unclean woman was to share in her defilement. Nevertheless, the woman is determined to stretch out her hand and touch the hem of Jesus's garment. "If I do this," she thinks to herself, "I will be made well." As soon as she touches Jesus the wellspring of blood in her is dried up, she is healed, and she feels it. But Jesus too feels something—the healing power going out of him. Jesus turns and asks, "Who touched me?" His disciples tease him and ask him how he could possibly be looking for one person who had touched him among the surging throng. Jesus keeps peering around, and the woman comes forward and "tells him the whole truth." Instead of rebuking the woman for making him unclean, Jesus tells her, "Daughter, your faith has made you well."

You could say that the woman was desperate, and that her circumstances had driven her to risk touching Jesus. Jesus's words, however, refocus our thinking; yes, he felt healing power emanate from himself, but he also recognized that the power of faith in the woman had been working too. In Ruby Sales's way of putting it, the woman loved herself enough to dare to act, and the act brought healing.

So far in these concluding remarks I've been concentrating on King and the power of overflowing love that aided him to see the "low-hovering" clouds of his day as truly being birth pangs of the Beloved Community. When I visited Thich Nhat Hanh in Vietnam in the Spring of 2019, I had an experience that speaks to the same power—that of love—still working in him, despite his advanced age and the stroke that robbed him of speech and the power to write or walk.

One of the young nuns at the convent next to the monastery where Nhat Hanh lives said to me with shining eyes, "I am privileged to be here now while Thay is conducting a revolution without words." The revolution she spoke of is the work of promoting gender equity, work Nhat Hanh began before his exile in 1966. It may strain your credulity to believe that Nhat Hanh could still be carrying on this work of gender equity from such a weakened state, but the young nun saw and believed it; so do I. It is the power of overflowing love working in Nhat Hanh, it is that he can touch, as he has said, the ultimate within himself in any moment; it is the power that comes from loving yourself.

Appreciating the reality and potency of the life within, especially the value of apprehending the presence of overflowing love that abides within you, is essential in the work of repairing the Beloved Community; without knowing that the "strong force" of the universe fully resides within, one may be more easily manipulated and used, as Ruby Sales has said. One might also give way to sadness and hopelessness unbuoyed by love in the soul. All the above being true, it is not the life of the hermit ascetic that is recommended. "Community" remains an irreducible value of the Beloved Community, a truth blazoned in the name itself— Beloved Community.

King and Nhat Hanh, in their friendship, their brotherhood, recapitulated in miniature the whole Beloved Community. But perhaps you are not convinced. Still, even at the end of this book, it would be fair to wonder: how can we call this slight collection of encounters and communications a friendship, a brotherhood? We know of people who work closely together and who share common purposes, but who would not put these work relationships into the category of friendship. We may also think of friendship as being something that builds over time, with the accumulation of shared experiences. A handful of letters and personal encounters, mutual support over a great cause, and a shared world citizenship—can this all add up to a friendship? And why would it matter if Nhat Hanh and King were truly friends or simply people with a shared mission?

Much has been made in this book about the importance of interconnection. What is essential, though, is not only the fact that all things are connected but also the quality of those connections. The two great universe models that came together when Nhat Hanh and King moved consciously into each other's circle—one model coming from a Buddhist lineage, and the other, the Beloved Community—springing originally from Christianity, recognize not only that interrelatedness is a feature of the world but also that the quality of that interrelatedness is love. Love in Nhat Hanh's model of reality manifests as compassion for all life; in King's model, as agape love.

Royce and all those who have followed him in the lineage of the Beloved Community valued love—specifically agape love— as a constituent part of what makes the Beloved Community. Royce put forward the circle of Jesus and his closest disciples as the Beloved Community in miniature, and the essential quality of the friendship in the Gospel descriptions of this intimate circle of Jesus's followers is agape.

In the course of my interviews with Sister Chan Khong, I asked her if Nhat Hanh's model of the universe (which she shared, being trained in the same lineage) could be both a description of reality-as-it-is and an image of the perfected state of the world when all are enlightened. In response, she said that more important than the fact that all things are connected, the model helps us to see that the Buddha is compassion and resides at the heart of all beings.

So, to return to the question of what makes the relationship between King and Nhat Hanh one that should be recognized as a friendship, and not simply a fruitful, fortuitous collaboration, it is, first, that they both held dear the quality of overflowing love, or, as Sister Chan Khong named it, compassion, and that the warmth of this love is palpable in their relationship. It is love that makes us friends with one another, not convenience or utility.

The deeply interconnected, holistic model of reality that is the Beloved Community, like other similar models, is truer to life than the mechanistic, industrial model. The exploration of the *community* part of Beloved Community, through its embodiment in the friendship between Nhat Hanh and King—has several things to teach us of substantive hope for the perilous moment we are in and the more difficult future that lies ahead.

To align with the holistic model of the universe is to begin to live in loyalty to life as it is. Loyalty to the Beloved Community turns into protection of the parts that make up the community and of the community itself. The immense energies of people loyal to the Beloved Community will more and more be brought to bear on behalf of the community and its members. The working out of loving loyalty to the Beloved Community will help, in the furthest reaches of such efforts, prevent our becoming forlorn passengers on Spaceship Earth operating in life-support mode, a terrible fate as James Lovelock pointed out.[*]

The International Panel on Climate Change, an advisory committee of the United Nations, issued in 2018 a comprehensive report on the progress or lack thereof on the goals of the Paris Agreement. It was widely publicized and commented upon, and,

---

[*] James Lovelock is the originator of the Gaia theory on the self-maintaining quality of the earth's biosphere. He takes on the popular expression "spaceship Earth" as implying a terrifying, not hopeful possible future: when we have extracted all the fossil fuels, eradicated species beyond the tipping point of maintaining healthy ecosystems (of which we are a part), poisoned the earth and our bodies to a dangerous level, it is a pathetic expedient to then treat the earth as a spaceship that will carry the remnant of humanity until we can find a habitable planet to colonize.

in many cases, misunderstood. Perhaps the most famous bit from the report is an estimated time window of twelve years for climate action to keep warming below 1.5°C above pre-Industrial levels. Among the misconceptions that have clustered around this bare number is the idea that we have all the way to the end of the twelve-year period, almost like a death-bed confession, in order to make the transformation needed—that if we start working very, very hard at climate action toward the end of the twelve-year period, we'll make it. This is not true, for the policies and practices that would shape such ardent climate action have a much greater lead time; some estimates say that the necessary policy work needs to happen in the first few years after the IPCC report was issued; that is between 2020 and 2022, for useful climate action to take place within the twelve-year time frame.

"Living in alignment with life," as I've suggested, perhaps by setting in motion what I've begun calling Beloved Community Circles[144] (described more specifically in the following section) may be inherently healthy, but may not be enough to stave off disaster. Let us take the challenge of social structural change— for example, what is the point of creating patient, long-term, dispersed circles if their work can't be accomplished in time to prevent climate chaos? The best answer I can give is twofold. First, it is better, existentially, to live in alignment with what is true than it is to perpetuate a false and destructive model. Second, and equally important: Beloved Community Circles would become reservoirs of health, courage, and wisdom during times of climate chaos and its attendant social disruption. I drew upon the imperative of aligning with that which is true, together, during a Holy Week sermon in 2019. At that time, I preached to the assembled clergy of the Episcopal Diocese of California about the role our congregations and institutions might play as the number of climate refugees swells. People who live the reality of interbeing within the Beloved Community may help others live with less fear.

The Beloved Community is projected in full by every cell of the whole; this is the teaching of interbeing, of interpenetration that Thich Nhat Hanh brought into the understanding of the Beloved Community. Interpenetration (and interconnectedness too) seems pure fancy if we are used to looking only through the lens of the mechanistic, industrial model. Those who, due to loyalty, endure within the experiential life of the Beloved Community come to know the truth of interconnectedness.

It is because of this principle of fullness being expressed by the presence of even the smallest member of the Beloved Community that we see such great power for reconciliation and healing flowing from individual acts such as the self-immolation of Thich Quang Duc, the martyrdom of King, or the life-long dedication and sacrifice of Nhat Hanh. As Muste wrote, "Thus it is that whenever love that will suffer unto death is manifested . . . unconquerable power is released into the stream of history."[145] Interbeing would understand and affirm Muste's Christian statement. There is substantial hope, then, in Beloved Community Circles and the like; they may seem quixotic from the standpoint of the dominant model, but each cell can project into reality the Beloved Community.

And what about the divine origin of the Beloved Community and the role of prayer? We have watched Nhat Hanh wrestle with the notion of a personal God—so central and foundational a reality for King. The outcome, for me, of Nhat Hanh's love-motivated striving is a saying "yes" to the existence of a personal God, but a God greatly removed from ordinary conceptions of the same. A God with personhood is able to act, to meet and help the individual and the community. For those who seek to be loyal to the Beloved Community in their life, prayer is a commendable part of their daily practice. Prayer is an antidote to egotism, to the delusion that all depends on our own efforts. Great grief can pool up in one's heart, in the soul, and acts as a source of toxin; prayer can help channel that grief back to the ocean of love, whence comes healing. And prayer invokes divine aid in the struggle.

The bodhisattvas who have been removed from our midst by martyrdom are with us still to awaken us, to support us, to encourage us, and to continue their own work. In the words of the author of the New Testament Letter to the Hebrews,

> *Therefore, since we are surrounded by so great a cloud of witnesses, let us also lay aside every weight and the sin that clings so closely, and let us run with perseverance the race that is set before us.*[146]

In my research, I have learned from Nhat Hanh to look for the living presence of those who have died. Their help—real in the same way that pious Catholics view the help of the saints—is something I felt in an unorganized, uninformed way as I began this research. Now I have begun to look, as Nhat Hanh says, intently and with ardor for their presence. I feel that Jonathan Daniels was present with us that day in Hayneville, Alabama, when I hosted the annual Jonathan Daniels and the Martyrs of Alabama Pilgrimage and when Representative John Lewis spoke at the service at the close of the day. The spiritual experiences of that day were answers to an unvoiced, unconscious prayer.

The Beloved Community grows and moves toward fulfillment. I have spent some time writing about the mutuality of reconciliation stretching from the present to the past, and in reverse. It is also possible to see the arc of mutuality stretching toward the future. Pierre Teilhard de Chardin, the eminent twentieth-century paleontologist and Jesuit priest, posited a holistic, interconnected, planetary model that is in motion toward an Omega point, a place of maximal complexity, integration, and fulfillment.

When I was a young priest, serving as a curate in a large suburban parish outside of Philadelphia, more than thirty years ago, I had one parishioner who would write me letters about my sermons. Dorothy Love Saunders was elderly and from a privileged Southern family, and who had—I don't know how this came to be—gone on her grand tour not to Europe but to the Middle East. By her own account, she was utterly unfamiliar with any religion but American, Southern Protestantism. She was on her tour during Ramadan, and the obvious faith of the Muslims she saw keeping their fasts shattered her easy assumptions about the superiority of Christianity. She became a spiritual and intellectual seeker. Her study had introduced her to Teilhard long before I came on the scene. I will never forget one of her beautifully penned letters, after a sermon in which I made an equivalency between evil during the time of Jesus and in our own day. In sum, I had said things hadn't gotten any better; perhaps, given population and technology, things were worse. She chided me for a lack of faith (in the genuinely nicest way), and went on to write that Christ is inexorably moving the world toward its completion and that this was true—outward appearances to the contrary. It was crucial, she wrote, to lend our conscious efforts to the divine energies of Christ, out of loyalty and love, because it is our best nature. Dorothy Love Saunders's message to me is the message of the Beloved Community, the beautiful reality tended to and explicated by King, taken up in loving friendship by Nhat Hanh, and—beyond him—given to us all. Nhat Hanh is releasing the leadership of the Beloved Community to us all. The responsibility for tending, healing, restoring, and fulfilling the Beloved Community is a fearsome gift, and one of infinite worth.

Several times in these closing comments I've referred to or quoted Jesus of Nazareth. If you have felt some resistance to these references, this is completely understandable. What was not a religion when Jesus proclaimed the nearness of the Beloved Community and called for people to furnish themselves with a new mind suited to the high demands of their day, within four hundred years had become the official religion of the Roman Empire. From the fourth century CE forward, Christianity somewhere on the planet has been the co-conspirator with empire, and in some guises, it remains so today. I am an ordained clergyperson within one of the three largest Christian bodies in the world, an institution that has been closely identified with two empires, the British Empire and the current American empire.

But my faith, based on deep experience of Jesus, the Christ, can welcome the Beloved Community. How do I understand the Beloved Community and the religions of Nhat Hanh and of King, Buddhism and Christianity, respectively? Nhat Hanh has said that he may know the Buddha and Jesus better than many people who lived in their circles during their earthly lives, for, he goes on, he visits Jesus and Buddha every day. It is sure that Nhat Hanh visits both of these great beings not to worship them but, as the late Marcus Borg said, to follow them; Borg was writing only of Jesus, but the same holds true for the Buddha. Maybe better even than "follow," we might say, "befriend."

The sangha and the Body to which the Buddha and Jesus pointed are both ways of speaking of the Beloved Community, an interrelated, peaceful community held together by overflowing love and compassion. The Beloved Community is cherished by Christians and Buddhists under other names, but neither religion, in fact no religion, possesses the Beloved Community.

If you are part of a religion, please stay loyal to that religion, but make it transparent to the Beloved Community—see the Beloved Community shimmering in its nearness within your sacred rites and in the loving circles of others who share your faith. If you are outside of religion, do not feel any pressure to become part of one, but please respect your spiritual self, your inner self, and nurture it with all the love and creativity you can muster. And for each of you, save some of your energy—your intelligence, your knowledge and wisdom, your bodily energy and skill—for the work of repairing, building, and maintaining the Beloved Community.

Appendix:
Beloved Community Circles

During the "second wave" of the Covid-19 pandemic that bloomed noxiously in the late winter of 2020, some people, such as the Governor of California, Gavin Newsom, began referring to a "twindemic." Newsom meant the Covid-19 virus outbreak and the unprecedented wildfires raging through California and the Pacific Northwest, a sign of climate change. Earlier that summer, we also witnessed and took part in a rising consciousness about race in the United States. Black, Brown and Indigenous people in the United States have had a terrifying reality pressed upon them again and again over a 400-year period: white supremacy has extended and maintained its grip on the diverse populations of the United States with whatever force necessary. After the deaths of George Floyd, Breonna Taylor, and Ahmaud Arbery, just the most recent Black people who were murdered in acts of police violence, it seems that the consciousness scales of the nation had tipped. Whites in increasing numbers were grappling with personal, familial, community, and national histories, owning up to truths that had been hidden in plain sight.

The tidal wave of change that Josiah Royce foresaw in the early years of the twentieth century, and the continued ebbing of organized religion have advanced, each in different directions. Faced with the burgeoning ills of the present time, and with religion (and government, it must be admitted) less and less able to respond, what path forward lies before us? If we have been stirred by Nhat Hanh and King's loyalty to one another as brothers in the Beloved Community, and their loyalty to the Beloved Community itself, perhaps we can accept the gift Nhat Hanh has given us of responsibility for this universal communion of love and peace. Leadership of, loyalty to the Beloved Community will take courage, preparation, and skill. It will require the mindfulness that Nhat Hanh has spent decades teaching the world; it will require the nonviolent tactics of King; and it will require unflinching analysis of our history and our current state of being.

Importantly and perhaps surprisingly, the dispersed leadership, commonly held, of the Beloved Community will not mean abandoning the religious commitments one might already have, although it will likely mean the transformation of those commitments. It is a commonplace that for greater structures to arise, smaller ones must be abandoned. Royce, in laying the groundwork for understanding the Beloved Community, disagreed: it is possible, perhaps even healthy, to maintain the commitments, the vows, one has already sworn to, and at the same time to open oneself to a greater reality. King, in his embrace of a friendship with Nhat Hanh, was modeling this concept of holding on/embracing upward. Nhat Hanh, as we have seen, has explored Christian theology while holding fast to his grasp and teaching of a lively Buddhist dharma. What lies beyond even Nhat Hanh's understanding of the Beloved Community? How can we today unveil further truths about the Beloved Community and so meet the challenges that imperil the world?

I am calling the organizations that would help us make the structural changes we need Beloved Community Circles, with characteristics that include diversity, practices that "raise the tension" and are scalable for action, connections across geographic boundaries using web-based technologies, and norms that cultivate compassion, agape love, and learning.

What follows are thoughts about how we might actualize Beloved Community Circles, based on the life and teaching of Nhat Hanh and King, brothers in the Beloved Community. What might these Circles look like? What will they enable, across possible divides? Walking the path of pilgrimage, beginning decades ago when I had a burning call to learn more about Beloved Community, brings to mind what we might be together.

Beloved Community Circles Supporting Transformation

Beloved Community Circles will be deliberately diverse from inception of each circle. The model here is the Freedom Circles of the Church of the Savior in Washington, DC. There is only one Freedom Circle left, which is a pity, as the mission statement is so bracingly inspiring: "to overcome our cultural addiction to white male domination by the use of the twelve-step program in small circles whose membership is intentionally diverse."[147] By "intentionally diverse," the Church of the Savior means that membership is diverse from the offset and not revised after the initial membership is set. "Diverse" might look different in different settings.

For instance, when we do antiracism training in the Episcopal Church in the Bay Area of California, we look at diversity along many lines: gender, sexual orientation, income level, and race and ethnicity including Black, various groups that make up "Asian," Indigenous communities, and the various groups lumped under "Latino/Latina." The overall guideline on diversity for our Episcopal congregations is that we will strive to make our congregations as diverse as the neighborhood in which the church building is located. What is most important is recognizing the need to create diverse Beloved Community Circles.

Another category of diversity that deserves separate treatment is religious diversity. I have argued that King and Nhat Hanh's friendship is a seed of the Beloved Community, an embodiment of interbeing in part because they became friends despite what seem to be high barriers, one of which was their differing religious allegiances. We can guess that when Nhat Hanh and King met for the last time, in the phenomenal world in Geneva, and discussed the importance of building community to achieve their common goal of social change, the image they had of those communities was that they would be like their friendship—bridging many divisions, not the least of which was the religious divide.

The Freedom Circles achieved diversity within a religion—Christianity. Similarly, the Taizé Community in France attracts tens of thousands of Christian young people from around the world each summer, young people coming from many different Christian denominations, many of whom go back to their home countries and their home churches with their original religious commitments intact but with a broadened respect and appreciation for other ways of being Christian. Will Keepin and Cynthia Brix's interspirituality movement, though, indicates a path *between* religions, a useful way for thinking about creating Beloved Community Circles.

Brix and Keepin call their movement "interspirituality," distinct from interfaith. Interfaith might be described as cooperation between adherents of different religions; interspirituality is finding, exploring, and inhabiting a spiritual reality that lies among religions. Those who join Keepin and Brix in these interspirituality explorations are noted exponents of particular religious traditions, and they do not leave those traditions behind after tasting a spiritual reality that exists among, and yet apart, from identified religions.

For instance, the most senior nun in Tibetan Buddhism, the Venerable Jetsunma Tenzin Palmo, has taken part in Keepin and Brix's interspirituality retreats. Palmo, born in England in 1943, tested and tempered her mind by living in a Himalayan cave for twelve years, from 1976 to 1988.[148] During an interspirituality retreat in Costa Rica in 2018, Palmo was at ease with Christians, Sufis, Hindus, and Jews, yet afterward she continues as a Buddhist nun.

The Beloved Community embraces far more than the adherents of the world's religions—the Beloved Community is co-extensive with the world. Thus, Beloved Community Circles will form with people from all religions and from people who are areligious. Today, more and more people identify as "spiritual but not religious," the "nones" (from the polling category of "none" under the question, "What religion are you"). "Nones" will be as important as the nuns when forming Beloved Community Circles.

Beloved Community Circles will have a spiritual base and practices. King believed in the Beloved Community and it spiritual dimensions. King's outward-looking, prophetic, engaged Christianity planned and enacted social action— protests, boycotts, mass rallies—and he also believed that we need to recognize the interconnected nature of the world, the existence of a holistic model for the world—the Beloved Community—and that a personal God is the origin and sustaining force of the Beloved Community.

These foregoing belief statements, in order to be consequential, need to be rooted in spiritual practices, to move beyond the theoretical to the practical. Alongside the well-traveled routes of prayer, meditation, and ritual cultivated in the world's religions, the fruits of many centuries of religious development, Beloved Community Circles will be sustained by personal spiritual practices that are the fruit of individual creativity. Hospital workers who light a candle and dance before going to meet palliative and chronic-care patients: an elder who collects one beautiful fall leaf on her daily walk, arranges it and all the others on an heirloom plate she was given by her mother many years before, and in the spring, gently slides all the now-faded leaves back to the earth to provide the nourishment for the new growth of leaves budding; the young adult who draws a tarot card each morning and meditates on what it portends for the day that stretches ahead—all of these are real examples of how "nones" have created their own spiritual practices. How rich the mix will be in Beloved Community Circles when those supported by traditional practices meet and share with those forging their own ways of being spiritual.

Further fuel for the shape and content of the Beloved Community Circles comes from the example of Howard Thurman. As we have seen, leadership of mass gatherings was not the path Thurman chose. Though he explicitly advocated for direct nonviolent action to overturn stubbornly entrenched, oppressive systems, he gave his own energy for the formation of what is considered the first intentionally interfaith church in the United States, in 1944.[149] It is not surprising that Thurman chose this path, rather than one of movement leadership, as the "quest for community was the central category of his life and thought."[150] If we are to take up the mantle of the Beloved Community, we will need to build diverse communities, including the category of religious diversity.

Beloved Community Circles will be engaged in practices that "raise the tension" in the dominant political and economic system. Without eschewing mass demonstrations and marches, these groups will coordinate with other circles and with allies across lines of racial, economic, and cultural diversity to stage boycotts and to practice policy advocacy in local, state, and national legislative bodies. While the Beloved Community Circles are rooted locally, meeting in person regularly, they are linked to one another for the amplification of their political reach. Raising the tension was a key term in King's program for nonviolent action.

Another look at Thurman can clarify how Beloved Community Circles might participate in nonviolent action that raises the tension. As Dixie and Eisenstadt wrote of Thurman,

> One cannot always wait for the moral consciences of those in power to slowly awake from their slumbers. "To wait for moral pressure to work its perfect work may be too late. The oppressed may be annihilated meanwhile." . . . But if (and when) moral suasion fails, something Thurman called "shock" or the "shock method" must be tried. He told his audience in St. Louis that shock could be accomplished by "organizing a boycott, by organizing noncooperation, by engineering non-violent strikes." This was necessary because people in power "do not voluntarily, my friends, relinquish their hold on their place without being uprooted."[151]

The Beloved Community Circles need to be small enough to promote intimacy and person-to-person relationships, but in order to raise the tension and create the shock that will be needed, coordination for scale of action will be necessary. Beloved Community Circles will be connected to one another, including across national borders via the internet. While the detriments of the multiform, burgeoning, rapidly changing, internet-based world of communications have been catalogued by many, Beloved Community Circles would be able, through the internet, to maintain meaningful planning connections with international partners in ways that would not have been possible in King's lifetime.

Paul Hawken, in his book *Blessed Unrest*, compares the sprawling, numerous population of nongovernmental organizations (NGOs) in the world as functioning like the Earth's immune system.[152] Like our immune system, Hawken claims, a single NGO is like a single white blood cell—it does its healthful work without "knowing" what the other white blood cells are doing. Together, the white blood cells work remarkably well to keep the body healthy. While there are associations of NGOs within the whole population of NGOs, and though there is benefit from such associations, the overall good-functioning of the earth's immune system is not dependent on system-wide communication. Nevertheless, it is hard to imagine that the functioning of this global network would not be enhanced by technology-based communication that allows for coordination, mutual support, learning, planning, and amplified advocacy. We can learn to think and act both locally and globally.

Beloved Community Circles will cultivate compassion and agape love. This applies among members of circles as well as outward-radiating patterns, embracing neighborhoods, cities, and ecosystems in which human communities are nested. Long-term, small, face-to-face, diverse groups that meet regularly present good opportunities to learn the content of one another's lives, and so to move into I-Thou relationships, subject to subject. Practicing deep listening within the Beloved Community Circles will help participants overcome the alienation endemic to a culture overtaken by the machine model of the industrial and technology cultures.

Beloved Community Circles will be learning communities. Royce, as I have laid out earlier, defined part of the "problem" of Christianity as being the coming flood of technological innovation, matched by the continued decline of the power and vitality of religious bodies. Social change has accompanied technological change. The contemporary practice of nonviolence needs to be nimble with respect to meeting the rapidly changing conditions of human cultures today. Beloved Community Circles will need to take on board not only the lessons of earlier nonviolent movements but also new material that allows appropriate response to the demands of today.

One of the most remarkable features of the King–Nhat Hanh friendship is that each came to the friendship as an adherent and interpreter of a worldview characterized by complexity and integration. Thus, when they had their last conversation in the phenomenal world in 1967 and agreed on the prime importance of building communities for the work of social justice, the conversation was ripe for synergy, the productive bringing together of two great theoretical systems for the purpose of practical community formation. We have seen that more than an abstract discussion of the importance of community formation, the conversation in Geneva was the occasion for the transmission of the Beloved Community concept from King to Nhat Hanh. In possession of a robust vision of an interconnected, interpenetrating world, Nhat Hanh was poised to make creative contributions to the Beloved Community, contributions explored in this book.

With regard to the Beloved Community Circles, what contribution can Nhat Hanh's school of Buddhism make to their formation? Nhat Hanh's Buddhism helps us see that some of the potential power of Beloved Community Circles will lie in perceiving each circle as manifesting in itself the whole of the Beloved Community. Writing about the strand of Buddhism in which Nhat Hanh was trained, Yoshinori says,

> [It] is not merely a matter of epistemological or psychological transformation, teaching only a new way to see the world which remains unchanged. Since the radical transformation or turnabout (parāvṛtti) in enlightenment experience involves both the subject and object, both the self and the world undergo transformation.[153]

So, as Beloved Community Circles deepen their practices, the whole Beloved Community is being itself healed and restored.

And in reverse, the great, full Beloved Community lends its healing power to each cell, each Beloved Community Circle. The great Buddhist Patriarch Yoshinori saying intimates the star-tling—to a mind not conditioned by interbeing—concept that each part of a whole has the power to project or create the whole.

So here is some ground for hope: small communities project the whole Beloved Community. Even, in fact, individuals who, deprived of access to communities of mutual support, yet pattern their lives by the principles of the Beloved Community and are loyal to it, project the whole Beloved Community. There are, it must be said, countless instances of such small communities and isolated but loyal individuals; the proposed Beloved Community Circles would only be a new expression of the Beloved Community. The intentionality and loyalty to the Beloved Community by the Beloved Community Circles would be a positive contri-bution to the overall "immune system" of the earth. Never doubt the power of even the smallest effort to maintain and heal the Beloved Community, know always that great beings join you in your effort to repair the Beloved Community, and, finally, know that the Beloved Community itself lends you its divine aid.

Forming the Beloved Community Circles

If you are inspired to create a Beloved Community Circle, you might wonder how to get started. Here are a few simple ideas and guidelines to help you:

- Stretch yourself outside your circle of friends. The example of Taizé services as they are enacted in the United States can be a lesson about this principle. Taizé is an ecumenical Christian monastic community in the Burgundy region of France that attracts many thousands of young adults to live in community for a week at a time during the summer of each year. Their services, lit by votive candles, with icons around the room, and especially their distinctive body of chant music have become popular all over the world, and certainly in the United States. There are two marked differences, though, between many of the US Taizé-style services and what you would experience at the community in France: First, the services in France are not only ecumenical in concept, but also the group that gathers for the week-long sessions come from many faiths, many countries. In the US, most Taizé services are attended by people who are already part of the host congregation. And secondly, the Taizé community has a purpose, a goal: to promote reconciliation between divided communities and nations. Let the Taizé model be your guide—invite people who represent races, religions, political parties, genders, sexual orientations different than your own.

- Start small. Just invite one or two people to begin. Then, invite these initial members of the circle to invite one or two. Cap your circle at seven or eight people. Are there more interested? Help them start a new circle, and link your circles together!

- Establish the principles of nonviolence and reconciliation for your circle from the beginning.

- Agree on a common spiritual practice to open and close each meeting. It should be substantive, but not "owned" by any one religious tradition. Perhaps open with an expression of gratitude at the beginning, and close with a prayer; the Serenity Prayer might be a healthy way to move out into the world from within your circle. A substantial period of silence within the group is also of great value.

In closing, know that I pray that the Beloved Community exemplified in the life of Martin Luther King Jr. and Thich

Nhat Hanh will be a blessing in your life as well. Their friendship, their brotherhood, and their lives have been transformative in our world. May we all know the source of overflowing love and create space for creative and compassionate Beloved Community.

Gratitude

Professor Robert McDermott, California Institute of Integral Studies (CIIS), told me that I had been entrusted with the theme of this book by the bodhisattvas Martin Luther King Jr. and Thich Nhat Hanh. While I do not have a sense of deserved-ness about being entrusted with this precious story, I also do not doubt the truth of his insight. Let me, then, begin my expressions of gratitude to Martin and Thay: I have felt your support throughout.

There are other great beings—both famous and more intimately loved—who have taught me and helped me on this particular path, but who are no longer with us on this plane of life: Professor Jay Kim (University of Tennessee), the Rev. Bob Brooks, Professor Vincent Harding, Sister Maurus Allen, OSB, Brother Roger of Taizé, Congressman John Lewis, the Rev. Deacon Adele Stockham, the Rev. Marc Waldo, Anne Waldo, and the Rev. Canon Stefani Schatz.

My mother, Mary Frances Andrus, died during the intense period of my dissertation research and writing. Sheila and I were in Greece, taking part in a climate change symposium hosted by His All Holiness the Ecumenical Patriarch, at the time of her death. Mary Frances taught me essentials in life, like sharing with me her favorite passage of the Bible: "And what does the Lord require but to do mercy, seek justice and walk humbly with my God." When asked by our youngest daughter what her grandmother's favorite color was, Mary Frances immediately answered, "Green, because you always have to keep growing." She said this from a hospital bed where she was recovering from emergency heart surgery.

And to those who continue to journey with us on the earthly pilgrimage of all life: the Rev. Canon Vincent Strudwick (Oxford University emeritus), the Rev. Kerry Holder, Zara Renander, Catherine Flowers, Fannie Davis, Vandiver Chaplin, Ruby Sales, and Tom Poynor.

Special mention and gratitude must be made to the faculty of the Department of Philosophy, Cosmology and Consciousness at CIIS and the graduate students who were my colleagues. CIIS is closely woven into the history of progressive, visionary California through the 1960s and up to this moment. Among that remarkable faculty, my dissertation committee, Professor Jacob Sherman (Chair) and Professor Robert McDermott, joined by eminent Stanford historian Professor Clayborne Carson, helped me through the research and draft after draft of the dissertation itself. I can honestly say that every step, every iteration, brought pleasures and revelations, yet I know that for the committee, and especially Jacob and Robert, within CIIS, my dissertation represented an immense amount of work; I think of you all with thankfulness so often.

My deep gratitude to the good people of the Diocese of Alabama, who called me to a place of witness for civil rights, and to the extraordinary Diocese of California, especially my colleagues on diocesan staff and the elected diocesan leadership—you have supported and cheered me on through the decade of my doctoral work at CIIS and on to this book.

My editor, Jacob Surpin, and all the staff of Parallax Press have been soulful, professional colleagues. Thank you and I look forward to the future!

Thanks to my own brothers in the Beloved Community, Owsley Brown, and the Most Reverend Michael Bruce Curry.

Finally, gratitude to my family: Sheila, Pilar, Chloé, and Martin, my sister Babette Foster and her family, my sister-in-law Charlette Moore and her family, our godson Lee Tate and his family, and Gail and Perry Epes. I am enormously blessed by each and all of you.

Notes

1 Sister Chan Khong, *Learning True Love: Practicing Buddhism in a Time of War* (Berkeley, CA: Parallax Press, 1993), 25–26.

2 Thich Nhat Hanh (trans. Mobi Warren), *Fragrant Palm Leaves: Journals, 1962–1966* (New York: Riverhead Books, 1998), 7.

3 Nhat Hanh, *Fragrant Palm Leaves*, 60.

4 Khong, *Learning True Love*, 25–26.

5 Khong, *Learning True Love*, 48–49.

6 Khong, *Learning True Love*, 49.

7 Khong, *Learning True Love*, 50.

8 Debbie Elliott, "After MLK's Death, Coretta Scott King Went to Memphis to Finish His Work," NPR: All Things Considered, April 8, 2018, *https://www.npr.org/2018/04/08/597703360/after-mlks-death-coretta-scott-king-went-to-memphis-to-finish-his-work*.

9 Melissa Block, "Martin Luther King Recording Found in India," NPR: All Things Considered, January 16, 2009, *https://www.npr.org/templates/story/story.php?storyId=99480326*.

10 Plato, *The Apology of Socrates*, 30d–31a.

11 Martin Luther King Jr., "Martin Luther King Jr.—Acceptance Speech," Nobel Prize.org, accessed August 20, 2021, *https://www.nobelprize.org/prizes/peace/1964/king/26142-martin-luther-king-jr-acceptance-speech-1964/*.

12 Drew Dellinger, "The Mountaintop Vision: Martin Luther King's Cosmology of Connection" (PhD diss., California Institute of Integral Studies, 2012), abstract, *https://drewdellinger.org/dissertation-abstract__the-mountaintop-vision/*.

13 Josiah Royce, *The Problem of Christianity* (Washington, DC: The Catholic University of America Press, 2001), Kindle location 4244.

14 Gary Herstein, "The Roycean Roots of the Beloved Community," *The Pluralist* 4, no. 2 (Summer 2009): 91–107, *https://www.jstor.org /stable/20708980.*

15 Galatians 3:28 (New Revised Standard Edition).

16 We all remember that the apostle Paul conceived human history as including a process of education. As "modern man" of his own time, the apostle conceived himself to have become able to read the lesson of this process. But such a postulate, whether true or false, whether asserted in Paul's time or in our own, whether Christian in its formulation or not, includes a doctrine that will later occupy a large place in our inquiry—the doctrine that the human race, taken as a whole, has some genuine and significant spiritual unity so that its life is no mere flow and strife of opinions but includes a growth in genuine insight. Royce, *Problem of Christianity*, locations 533, 541.

17 Royce, *Problem of Christianity*, locations 421, 430.

18 Karen Guth, "Reconstructing Nonviolence: The Political Theology of Martin Luther King Jr. after Feminism and Womanism," *Journal of the Society of Christian Ethics* 32, no. 1 (Spring/Summer 2001): 75–92.

19 Thich Nhat Hanh, *Love Letter to the Planet* (Berkeley, CA: Parallax Press, 2013), Kindle, 20. We must conclude that Nhat Hanh views all life on the Earth, a being he calls here "a great bodhisattva," as existing within the Beloved Community.

20 Royce, *Problem of Christianity*, locations 1432, 1441.

21 Royce, *Problem of Christianity*, locations 4094, 4102.

22 I Cor. 11:27–29 (NRSV).

23 I Cor. 11:30 (NRSV).

24 Royce specifies that the atoning agent could be the community itself, or else "a servant of the community in whom its Spirit fully dwells." Royce, *Problem of Christianity*, locations 275, 281.

25 Royce, *Problem of Christianity*, locations 3180–3216.

26 Royce, *Problem of Christianity*, locations 3180–3216.

27 The story in Acts 8, in which Peter and John go on a mission to the city of Samaria. Philip had been there previously, preaching and baptizing. Peter and John prayed for and laid hands on those who had been baptized because, "as yet they had not received the Holy Spirit." This progressive enlightening of the world is made possible by the Resurrection of Jesus, and the subsequent gift by God of the Holy Spirit for the world. The fourteenth chapter of the Gospel of John limns the arc: Jesus leaves this world, prays to his Father God, and God sends the Holy Spirit to the believers. John 14 (NRSV).

28 Herstein, "Roycean Roots," 96.
29 Walter Earl Fluker, "They Looked for a City: A Comparison of the Idea of Community in Howard Thurman and Martin Luther King, Jr.," *The Journal of Religious Ethics* 18, no. 2, (Fall 1990): 35–55.
30 Royce, *Problem of Christianity*, locations 1088–1097.
31 Royce, *Problem of Christianity*, location 1096.
32 Josiah Royce, *The Hope of the Great Community* (New York: The MacMillan Company, 1916): 44, 45.
33 Martin Ceadel, "Pacifism and Conscientious Objection," The British Library, January 29, 2014, *https://www.bl.uk/world-war-one/articles/pacifism*.
34 Paul Dekar, *Creating the Beloved Community: A Journey with the Fellowship of Reconciliation* (Telford PA: Cascadia Publishing House, 2005).
35 Jill Wallis, *Valiant for Peace: A History of the Fellowship of Reconciliation 1914 to 1918* (London: Fellowship of Reconciliation, London, 1991), 7.
36 Wallis, *Valiant for Peace*, 5.
37 Wallis, *Valiant for Peace*, 4, 5.
38 Wallis, *Valiant for Peace*, 10.
39 Walter Wink, introduction to "Pacifism and Class War," by A. J. Muste, in *Peace is the Way: Writings on Nonviolence from the Fellowship of Reconciliation*, ed. Walter Wink (Maryknoll, New York: Orbis Books, 2000). This book was a collection of articles drawn from Fellowship, the official publication of the Fellowship of Reconciliation.
40 Albert J. Raboteau, *American Prophets: Seven Religious Radicals and Their Struggle for Social and Political Justice* (Princeton, NJ: Princeton University Press, 2016), 53, 54.
41 Raboteau, *American Prophets*, 37.
42 Royce, *Problem of Christianity*, location 3180–3216.
43 A.J. Muste, "Pacifism and Class War," in *Peace is the Way*, ed. Walter Wink (Maryknoll, New York: Orbis Books, 2000), 48..
44 Martin Luther King Jr., "My Pilgrimage to Nonviolence," in *Peace Is the Way: Writings on Nonviolence from the Fellowship of Reconciliation*, ed. Walter Wink, (Maryknoll, NY: Orbis Books, 2000), 64–71. King's usage of "pacifist" with respect to Muste's lecture must mean active nonviolence, as he began the article saying that, "[D]uring my student days at Morehouse I read Thoreau's Essay on Civil Disobedience for the first time. Fascinated by the idea of refusing to cooperate with an evil system, I was so deeply moved that I reread the work several times. This was my first intellectual contact with

the theory of nonviolent resistance." Though King says at the end of the quotation, "nonviolent resistance," it seems that if he is consistent within the article, we should take the description of Thoreau's theme, "refusing to cooperate with an evil system," as being a more apt expression of what he took from Thoreau, and that from Muste he began learning the active form of nonviolent resistance.

45 Martin Luther King Jr., "My Pilgrimage to Nonviolence," 65.

46 Martin Luther King Jr., "My Pilgrimage to Nonviolence," 65.

47 Martin Luther King Jr., "My Pilgrimage to Nonviolence," 65–67.

48 Martin Luther King Jr., "My Pilgrimage to Nonviolence," 68.

49 Martin Luther King Jr., "My Pilgrimage to Nonviolence," 68–70.

50 Martin Luther King Jr., "My Pilgrimage to Nonviolence," 71.

51 "The Burning Monk, 1963," Rare Historical Photos, *https://rarehistoricalphotos.com/the-burning-monk-1963/*.

52 Thich Nhat Hanh, Open letter to Martin Luther King, Jr. on the self-immolations of Buddhist monks, June 1, 1965.

53 Khong, *Learning True Love*, 37.

54 Khong, *Learning True Love*, 38.

55 Khong, *Learning True Love*, 93–104.

56 Khong, *Learning True Love*, 38–39.

57 Sister Chan Khong, personal interview with author, June 12, 2019, Dieu Tram Nunnery, Hue, Vietnam.

58 Khong, personal interview.

59 Khong, *Learning True Love*, 37, 39.

60 Raboteau, *American Prophets*, 28.

61 "Medicine King," The Nichiren Buddhist Library, accessed August 20, 2021, *https://www.nichirenlibrary.org/en/dic/Content/M/81*.

62 James A. Benn, "Where Text Meets Flesh: Burning the Body as an Apocryphal Practice in Chinese Buddhism," *History of Religions* 37, no. 4 (1998): 295–322.

63 Nhat Hanh, *Fragrant Palm Leaves*, 172.

64 Nhat Hanh, *Fragrant Palm Leaves*, 146–147.

65 Nhat Hanh, *Fragrant Palm Leaves*, 6–7.

66 Raboteau, *American Prophets*, 48.

67 Matthew 5:3–12, part of what is called the Sermon on the Mount, and Luke 6:20–23, part of the Sermon on the Plain (NRSV).

68 Matthew 5:10a, 12b (NRSV).

69 Matthew 23:37–39, (NRSV).

70 Not only was Abraham Joshua Heschel's book, The Prophets (New York: Harper & Row, 1962), popular in seminary and scholarly circles, Heschel and King knew one another. In one of the iconic pictures from the Selma March in 1965, John Lewis is identified on the far left, King is in the middle, and Heschel is two to the right of King.

71 Heschel, *The Prophets*, 256.

72 Heschel, *The Prophets*, 256.

73 Heschel, *The Prophets*, 268.

74 Abraham Joshua Heschel, "Religion in a Free Society," in *The Insecurity of Freedom: Essays on Human Existence* (New York: Farrar, Straus & Giroux, 1959), 11–12.

75 Taylor Branch, *At Canaan's Edge: America in the King Years, 1965–68* (New York: Simon & Schuster Paperbacks, 2006), 421–22, 470.

76 Deuteronomy 34:4 (NRSV).

77 Martin Luther King Jr., "I've Been to the Mountaintop," address delivered at Bishop Charles Mason Temple, in ed. Carson and Shepard, *A Call to Conscience* (New York: Warner Books, 2001).

78 King, "I've Been to the Mountaintop."

79 Boston pastor Jack Mendelsohn took a several-month sabbatical from his church in Boston in 1966 to write *The Martyrs: Sixteen Who Gave Their Lives for Racial Justice*. King was two years away from his own martyrdom, but a look at Mendelsohn's account of civil rights activist and martyr Medgar Evers's last day shows how the narratives of the prophets' lives in the Hebrew scriptures, and perhaps most importantly, the life of Moses, was an underlying metaphoric frame. Mendelsohn recounts that Evers, without any specific threats, still took solemn farewell with his closest friends and, earlier that day, with his children and wife. He felt a sense of foreboding, borne out as he said a serious and slow goodbye to the friend who had given him a ride home. As he walked to his house, a sniper shot him, and he died on his doorstep. Like the classic prophets and like King later, he stayed resolute in his mission, even though he had an inner knowing that it would likely lead to a martyr's death. Jack Mendelsohn, *The Martyrs: Sixteen Who Gave Their Lives for Racial Justice* (New York: Harper & Row, 1966), 77–79.

80 Then Jesus told his disciples, "If any want to become my followers, let them deny themselves and take up their cross and follow me. For those who want to save their life will lose it, and those who lose their life for my sake will find it. For what will it profit them if they

gain the whole world but forfeit their life? Or what will they give in return for their life? Matthew 16:24–26 (NRSV).

81 Thich Nhat Hanh, "In Search of the Enemy if Man (addressed to Martin Luther King)," June 1, 1965, http://www.aavw.org/special_features/letters_Thich_abstract02.html.

82 Martin Luther King Jr., *The Trumpet of Conscience* (Boston: Beacon Press, 1967), 11–12.

83 Martin Luther King Jr., *"In a Single Garment of Destiny": A Global Vision of Justice*, ed. Lewis V. Baldwin (Boston: Beacon Press, 2013), Kindle location 3389.

84 Taylor Branch writes that the total meetings consumed most of the day (Branch, *At Canaan's Edge*, 470), but Nhat Hanh, in an interview with Oprah Winfrey, said that the private conversation lasted about 45 minutes), Oprah.com, "Oprah Talks to Thich Nhat Hanh," Oprah.com, March 2010, https://www.oprah.com/spirit/oprah-talks-to-thich-nhat-hanh/2.

85 Oprah.com, "Oprah Talks to Thich Nhat Hanh," Oprah.com, March 2010, https://www.oprah.com/spirit/oprah-talks-to-thich-nhat-hanh/2.

86 For instance, both the *Time* (Liam Fitzpatrick, "The Monk Who Taught the World Mindfulness Awaits the End of This Life, January 24, 2019) and the *New York Times* (Richard C. Paddock, "Thich Nhat Hanh, Preacher of Mindfulness, Has Come Home to Vietnam," May 16, 2019) articles about Nhat Hanh's return, in October 2018, to Vietnam, mention the Peace Prize nomination.

87 Timothy Joseph identifies Plato's *Apology* as the source of Socrates's use of "gadflies" who, by their bites, rouse the complacent Athenians to higher levels of awareness and action. Timothy Joseph, "Martin Luther King Jr. in Dialogue with the Ancient Greeks," *The Conversation*, February 1, 2016, https://theconversation.com/martin-luther-king-jr-in-dialogue-with-the-ancient-greeks-53550.

88 Thich Nhat Hanh, *At Home in the World: Stories and Essential Teachings from a Monk's Life* (Berkeley, CA: Parallax Press, 2019), 72.

89 Immediately the *Washington Post* and the *New York Times* published articles criticizing the speech, as did, from within the movement, the National Association for the Advancement of Colored People and civil rights activist Ralph Bunch. Martin Luther King Jr., "Beyond Vietnam," King Encyclopedia, The Martin Luther King, Jr. Research and Education Institute, Stanford University, accessed August 20, 2021, https://kinginstitute.stanford.edu/encyclopedia/beyond-vietnam.

90 King, "Beyond Vietnam."

91 King, *The Trumpet of Conscience*, 11.

92 Nhat Hanh, *At Home in the World*, 72.
93 Sister Chan Khong, personal interviews with author, June 12–16, 2019, Tu Hieu Patriarchal Monastery, Hue, Vietnam.
94 Nhat Hanh, *At Home in the World*, 73.
95 Thich Nhat Hanh, *Love in Action: Writings on Nonviolent Social Change* (Berkeley, CA: Parallax Press, 1993), 10.
96 Khong, *Learning True Love*, 93–94.
97 Khong, *Learning True Love*, 98, 99.
98 Khong, *Learning True Love*, 99.
99 Khong, *Learning True Love*, 105; and Nhat Hanh, *Love in Action*, 9.
100 Nhat Hanh, *Love in Action*, 9, 12.
101 Nhat Hanh, *Love in Action*, 25, emphasis mine.
102 Nhat Hanh, *Love in Action*, 13.
103 Nhat Hanh, *Love in Action*, 13.
104 Nhat Hanh, *Love in Action*, 35.
105 Nhat Hanh, *Love in Action*, 17.
106 Nhat Hanh, *Love in Action*, 27–28.
107 Nhat Hanh, *Love in Action*, 26.
108 Nhat Hanh, *Love in Action*, 29.
109 Nhat Hanh, *Love in Action*, 31–32.
110 Nhat Hanh, *Love in Action*, 31–32.
111 Nhat Hanh, *Love in Action*, 10.
112 Nhat Hanh, *Love in Action*, 10.
113 Nhat Hanh, *Love in Action*, 23.
114 Nhat Hanh, *Love in Action*, 23.
115 Nhat Hanh, *Love in Action*, 13.
116 Nhat Hanh, *Love in Action*, 32–34.
117 Thich Nhat Hanh, *No Death, No Fear: Comforting Wisdom for Life* (New York: Riverhead Books, 2002), 14.
118 Thich Nhat Hanh, "Practicing Listening with Empathy," *Buddhism Now*, April 23, 2014, *https://buddhismnow.com/2014/04/23 /practising-listening-with-empathy-by-thich-nhat-hanh/*.
119 Nhat Hanh, *No Death, No Fear*, 14.
120 Nhat Hanh, *No Death, No Fear*, 19–20.
121 Nhat Hanh, *No Death, No Fear*, 20.
122 Fred Eppsteiner, "Introduction" in Thich Nhat Hanh, *Interbeing: Fourteen Guidelines for Engaged Buddhism* (Berkeley, CA: Parallax Press, 1987).
123 Eppsteiner, "Introduction," xxvi.

124 Dan Tate, "Maximus the Confessor, Visionary of the Cosmic Christ," Christ and Cosmos, January 17, 2020, *https://www.christcosmos.com /blog/st-maximus-confessor-visionary-of-the-cosmic-christ-a-crash-course.*

125 "Thich Nhat Hanh," Deer Park Monastery, accessed August 20, 2021, *https://deerparkmonastery.org/thich-Nhat-hanh/.*

126 "Thich Nhat Hanh," Deer Park Monastery.

127 Nhat Hanh, *Fragrant Palm Leaves*, 6–7.

128 Nhat Hanh, *Fragrant Palm Leaves*, 6–7.

129 Thich Nhat Hanh, Interbeing..

130 Thich Nhat Hanh, *Going Home: Jesus and Buddha as Brothers* (New York: Riverhead Books, 1999), 5.

131 Thich Nhat Hanh, *The Heart of the Buddha's Teaching: Transforming Suffering into Peace, Joy, and Liberation* (New York: Harmony Books, 2015), 250–254.

132 Jim Forest, "A Few Memories of Thich Nhat Hanh," Jim & Nancy Forest, January 11, 2012, *https://jimandnancyforest.com/2012/01/ nhat-hanh/.*

133 Thomas Merton, "Nhat Hanh Is My Brother," Buddhist Door Global, accessed August 20, 2021, *https://www.buddhistdoor.net/ features/nhat-hanh-is-my-brother.*

134 David Steindl-Rast, foreword to Thich Nhat Hanh, *Living Buddha, Living Christ* (New York: Riverhead Books, 1995), Kindle locations 59, 67.

135 bell hooks, foreword to Daniel Berrigan and Thich Nhat Hanh, *The Raft Is Not the Shore: Conversations toward a Buddhist-Christian Awareness* (Maryknoll, NY: Orbis Books, 2001), vii.

136 Personal correspondence given to author by Deacon Vicki Gray.

137 Hannah Hindstrom, "The Rise of Buddhist Feminism?," *The Diplomat*, May 18, 2014, *https://thediplomat.com/2014/05/ the-rise-of-buddhist-feminism/.*

138 Thich Nhat Hanh, "The Next Buddha Will Be a Sangha," *Inquiring Mind Journal*, Spring 1994.

139 Ewert Cousins, *Christ of the 21st Century* (New York: Continuum Publishing Company, 1998) 7; Jessica Roemischer, "A New Axial Age: Karen Armstrong on the History—And the Future—of God," accessed August 20, 2021, *http://www.adishakti.org/_/a_new_axial_ age_by_karen_armstrong.htm.*

140 Joanna Macy, *World as Lover, World as Self* (Berkeley, CA: Parallax Press, 2007), Kindle location 1159–1162.

141 Macy, *World as Lover*, location 2125–2130.

142 See Carolyn Merchant, *The Death of Nature: Women, Ecology and the Scientific Revolution* (San Francisco: Harper Collins Publishers, 1980) for one influential account of the rise of the currently prevailing model of the world.

143 Sean Kelly, "Living in the End Times," para 8, Revelore Press, accessed August 22, 2021, *https://revelore.press/publications/living-in-end-times/*.

144 See appendix.

145 Raboteau, *American Prophets*, 28.

146 Heb. 12: 1 (NRSV).

147 The Church of the Savior is comprised of numbers of small house churches. Clusters of these house churches have names that point to their particular vocation within the whole that is Church of the Savior. The Freedom Circles are part of "Church of Christ, Right Now." See "The 'Scattered Community' of Churches," Inward/Outward Together, Church of Our Savior, Washington, DC, accessed August 22, 2021, *http://inwardoutward.org/churches/*.

148 Joyce Morgan, "Tibetan Buddhist Nun, Jetsunma Tenzin Palmo, Finds Peace of Mind in Unstable Times," *Sydney Morning Herald*, July 14, 2017, *https://www.smh.com.au/entertainment/tibetan-buddhist-nun-jetsunma-tenzin-palmo-finds-peace-of-mind-in-unstable-times-20170714-gxb9ue.html*.

149 Mathews F. Allen, "Howard Thurman: Paradoxical Pavior," *Journal of Negro History* 77, no. 2 (Spring 1992): 85.

150 Fluker, "They Looked for a City," 37.

151 Quinton Dixie and Peter Eisenstadt, *Visions of a Better World: Howard Thurman's Pilgrimage to India and the Origins of African American Nonviolence* (Boston: Beacon Press, 2011), 141.

152 Paul Hawken, *Blessed Unrest: How the Largest Social Movement in History Is Restoring Grace, Justice, and Beauty to the World* (New York: Penguin Books, 2007), 3, 141.

153 Taitetsu Unno, "Philosophical Schools-San-lun, T'ien-t'ai, and Hua-yen" in *Buddhist Spirituality*, ed. by Takeuchi Yoshinori (New York: Crossroad, 1993), 343–365.

PARALLAX PRESS, a nonprofit publisher founded by Zen Master Thich Nhat Hanh, publishes books and media on the art of mindful living and Engaged Buddhism. We are committed to offering teachings that help transform suffering and injustice. Our aspiration is to contribute to collective insight and awakening, bringing about a more joyful, healthy, and compassionate society.

View our entire library at parallax.org.